EAT!

YOU'LL GET HUNGRY

A Family Food Saga

SAM GUGINO

ISBN: 978-1-950043-60-6

Publishing services provided by Archangel Ink

To Anna and Russell Gugino

CONTENTS

ACKNOWLEDGEMENTS

To say this book wouldn't be possible without my mother, Anna Gugino, would be the all-time understatement. Not just her recipes, but her warmth, strength, stamina, and understanding. You were always welcome in Anna Gugino's house, no matter who you were.

Many thanks also go to my father, Russell Gugino, my siblings, Frank, Russell, and Maria, my Aunt Sandy, and my grandmother, our "nana."

I'd also like to acknowledge my Big Aunt Jo; her husband, Uncle Alphonso (Big Uncle Al); my Aunt Betty and her husband, Uncle Charlie; and my recipe testers: my nieces Dana and Katie Gugino, Caroline Eberle, and Jackie Collard. And my cousins Maryann Bolles and Therese Giglia.

My thanks as well to Jim Hummel, who drew illustrations for several of my food stories in the *San Jose Mercury News*, including the wonderful cover illustration of a Gugino family Thanksgiving dinner. And to Art Milner, a friend and writing mentor, who encouraged me to focus on family, food, and humor in my writing.

Finally, no amount of thanks is sufficient for my wife, Mary Lee Keane, for the incalculable amount of support, encouragement, and wisdom she's given me, not just for this book, but for just about everything I've done in the past forty-nine years.

INTRODUCTION

Food, as you will find out in the ensuing chapters, has always been important to my family. Whether it was a routine weekday dinner, a holiday feast, or a post-funeral lunch, food was the glue that held everything and everybody together. One of the biggest meals in memory was provided to my immediate family by my aunts and cousins after we returned from my father's funeral. It was as if the volume of food was designed to ease the hurt.

This combination of death and eating is not uncommon with Italians. I have noticed, for example, that many Mafia chieftains, like Paul Castellano, Carmine Galante, and Joey "Crazy Joe" Gallo, have been gunned down in or outside restaurants. This, I believe, is the Italian equivalent of a Viking dying with a sword in his hand so that he may enter the kingdom of Valhalla.

Cooking and eating and talking about cooking and eating took up a lot of time in my family, as was the case with many Italian Americans. Some years ago, my brother Russell told me of having a very traditional Italian meal with a man who grew up eating the same foods we ate. While savoring his repast, he turned to my brother and said, "This is better than sex." Perhaps this gives you an idea of the depth of feeling some Italians have for their cuisine. Since we never talked about sex in my family, I can only assume that we channeled those passions into our cooking and eating.

Though food dominated our lives, it never occurred to me that what we ate was of interest to anyone outside the family (which included the extended family of aunts, uncles, and cousins). As a matter of fact, I often felt embarrassed because we weren't eating what other people were eating. And, as with most ethnic groups, it was important to assimilate. (I even wanted to change my name to something more "American." My model was Stan Jones, a Hall of Fame lineman for the Chicago Bears. I thought Sam Jones sounded nice.) Sharing an artichoke with a fifth-grade classmate would not make this any easier.

There were a few incidents during my early years that made me think, however briefly, that maybe we weren't the only ones who ate weird food. I was shoveling snow—something we often did in Buffalo, NY, where I grew up—off a neighbor's driveway one Sunday to earn some pocket money. When I finished, I went inside to collect my fee. (In the 1950s and early 1960s, a shoveled backyard, driveway, and sidewalk could be had for the princely sum of $3.) Our neighbor was Jewish, as were many in the neighborhood before other Italians followed us. As I entered the kitchen, I was shocked to see my neighbor eating cold fish—probably smoked whitefish or herring. And it wasn't even Friday!

But it wasn't until I got to college that I really began to appreciate my culinary heritage. Perhaps nothing makes you yearn for good home cooking more than regular meals at a campus dining facility. Also, in talking to other people from diverse backgrounds, I came to realize just how boring some of their eating habits were. I recall sitting in the living room with a few fraternity brothers at the Delta Tau Delta fraternity house at the University of Pennsylvania. Somehow, the subject of food came up, and I began to talk about the foods we ate at home. Everyone listened with interest, and one person in particular, John Madden, was especially fascinated. A major reason for his keen interest was that his upper-class Anglo-Saxon background probably included little Italian food beyond pizza and spaghetti and meatballs.

The reaction of guests at our dinner table was another indicator of how special my family's meals were. Because my brothers Frank and Russell attended colleges in central New York, they often brought classmates home. I can't recall anyone who wasn't bowled over by Mom's cooking—both the quantity and quality. I think the feeling of warmth in our household was undeniable as well.

After twenty-one years of having someone else cook for me, I started to cook for myself when I was a senior in college and living in a townhouse with two roommates in Center City, Philadelphia. Faced with this new independence, I tried to figure out just where to begin. Then I remembered how Mom shopped and cooked. And little by little, I started to duplicate both. It wasn't long before I was able to produce an entire Sunday spaghetti dinner that tasted exactly like Mom's.

After graduation in 1970, I continued to get serious about cooking. During my frequent visits to Washington, DC, where Frank lived, we often talked about the lack of good Italian restaurants, as well as delis and shops that sold Italian food products, especially in Washington. We fantasized about opening our own *alimentaria*. Alas, in early 1975, like Frost's poem "The Road Not Taken," Frank took the more traveled road and stayed with his sales job. With the encouragement and support of my wife, Mary, whose birthday present to me a year earlier was my first cooking class, I took the road less traveled. I left my insurance job and entered The Restaurant School in Philadelphia, which had opened the year before.

Those were heady times for food and wine across the country. Alice Waters started her legendary restaurant, Chez Panisse, in 1971. Lawyers, doctors, teachers, and the like were leaving their conventional jobs and going into the restaurant business. (Waters was a former Montessori teacher. Her first chef, Jeremiah Tower, was an architect.)

The Restaurant School broadened my culinary horizons dramatically. Following graduation, I operated two critically successful restaurants as chef and manager. A *Philadelphia Inquirer* review of my first restaurant, Vincenzo's, was titled "Where they serve the best Italian food." After stints with two hotels as a food-and-beverage manager, I began writing seriously in 1983.

Back in 1981, again with Mary's encouragement, I took a humor writing course at Temple University taught by Art Milner. It was there that I wrote a story called, "Eat … You'll Get Hungry," which was about family dinner in the Gugino household. Art suggested that I concentrate on the three topics contained in that piece—food, family, and humor.

I developed most of my early stories from memory. I have always had a facility for remembering trivia. This came in handy on multiple-choice tests in school, where the instant recall of state capitals was thought to be important. It was also invaluable in thinking of the details contained in the family stories. Later, I picked the collective brains of my mother, my aunt Sandy, Frank and Russ, and my sister, Maria.

The first published story in what I loosely referred to as the "Family Eating Saga" appeared in the *Philadelphia Daily News* on December 14, 1983. It was about Aunt Sandy's cookies and was submitted as "Have a Cookie." But like 90 percent of my titles, it was changed by a copy editor and became "The Ghost of Cookies Past" because of its nostalgia and because it ran during the Christmas season. Subsequent articles appeared periodically over the next few years in the *Daily News* and the *San Jose Mercury News*, where I was food editor from 1989 to 1994. Some of the stories have been modified for this book, and many have new recipes added to them.

After several attempts at making *Eat! You'll Get Hungry* a reality, I finally made headway during and after the pandemic of 2020. I was also encouraged by my brother Frank, who, with no experience, wrote *Man of Salt*, a pretty darned good historical novel. And so, with the help of nieces, nephews, and cousins, who tested some of the recipes (and whose names appear in the Acknowledgments), here is, at last, *Eat! You'll Get Hungry*.

From left: Frank, Russ, and Sam on a typical winter day
on Fargo Avenue in Buffalo in the late 1950s

MOM, DAD, AND THE POLISH CHURCH WEDDING

It wasn't until after my father died (on Friday, May 13, 1966, the day before my senior prom) that I found out the real story of how my parents got together. On the three evenings of my father's wake at the Greco Funeral Home, Russ, Frank, and I took turns welcoming people while my mother, overcome with grief, sobbed on a nearby sofa, consoled by her mother and sister and a bottle of witch hazel for her weary eyes.

One evening, when Russ was the greeter, a man arrived whom Russ didn't recognize. "Did you work with my father?" Russ asked, having figured by his appearance that he wasn't a relative and knowing that none of us had ever met any of Dad's coworkers.

"No," the man responded. "I knew your father when he was married before."

Russ was stunned. Nobody had ever told any of his children that their father had been divorced. Before Russ could tell his siblings what he'd found out, Uncle Charlie, who had heard all this, pulled Russ aside and gave him a brief explanation of my father's earlier and, as it turned out, unwise marriage. He also swore Russ to silence. It wasn't until a few years later that I was told this secret by Frank, who somehow found out, along with my sister, Maria, before I did.

Divorce in 1945, when my parents were married, was still a big deal, especially if you were Catholic. And particularly if you wanted to get married again. So, how did Anna Giglia (Mom's birth name) and Russell Gugino overcome this obstacle?

The answer lies with Uncle Charlie, Mom's brother, and Uncle George, Dad's half-brother, who were very close friends long before this issue came up. After Dad's divorce, George and Charlie got the idea that Russ would be a good match for Anna, who had never married. George and Charlie either weren't thinking about the Catholic thing, or it fell under the heading of We'll Cross That Bridge When We Come to It.

While Anna and Russ did meet a few times, sparks did not exactly fly before Dad went overseas in World War II. (Dad was too old to be drafted into the army, so he enlisted in the navy and joined the Seabees, an elite construction battalion.) But before he left, Dad asked Mom if they could correspond while he was away. They did, and that's how they fell in love, or at least how Mom fell in love, as she described it to me. (I think Dad was already smitten before he left.)

But when they decided to get married after Dad came home, there was that one seemingly insurmountable problem of a divorced person being forbidden from getting married in a Catholic church. And Mom, a devout Catholic, insisted on a Catholic church wedding. (This isn't a problem if you are a sufficiently wealthy and famous Catholic, like Ted Kennedy, who got an annulment after twenty-five years of marriage and three children so that he could remarry.)

Thus, the wily and resourceful Charlie and George went to work to find a Catholic church in Buffalo, NY, where Russell Gugino and Anna Giglia could marry. Charlie and George knew, of course, that this meant a bribe of some sort. Despite a substantial Catholic population, George and Charlie struck out in Buffalo and started looking outside the city. They hit paydirt in Lackawanna, a small town south of Buffalo along Lake Erie, mostly known for its huge Bethlehem steel plant.

Unfortunately, the church they found was a Polish Catholic church. (The vast majority of Catholics in the Buffalo area were either Polish or Italian.) Still, that was good enough for Mom. Now she and Dad—no doubt with some assistance from Charlie and George— had to concoct a story about why two Italian Catholics from Buffalo were getting married in a Polish Catholic church outside of Buffalo, when neither of them had any connection to Lackawanna or Bethlehem Steel. Somehow, the families on both sides bought the story they came up with—or chose to buy it.

Though Mom never questioned the legitimacy of her marriage or her love for my father, she apparently did feel the need for some kind of penance for marrying a divorced man in violation of church doctrine. I say *apparently* because Mom refused to discuss or even acknowledge the issue with her children. And so, through twenty years of marriage, Mom, a reverent and devoted Catholic, who said her rosary twice a day, never took Communion, the apotheosis of her faith. At the mass for my father's funeral, her penance completed, Mom took Communion for the first time since before she got married.

I think the moral of this story, if there is one, is that love trumps dogma, though there is often a price to pay.

Back row, from left: Uncle Charlie, Dad, Uncle George
Front row, from left: Mom's cousin Millie, Mom, Aunt Sandy

EAT! YOU'LL GET HUNGRY

In our family, food was more than just something you ate. Mom cooked because she loved us. We ate because we loved her—and because my father threatened to lock us in the basement and feed us nothing but raw onions if we didn't. If you were sick, you ate. If you were well, you ate. If it was a rainy Tuesday, you ate. And if it was a holiday, you ate twice as much.

One of the worst insults my father could hurl at anyone was "You eat like a bird." (Yes, I'm aware that birds eat up to half their weight daily. But the image of a bird pecking at bits of food—even though it is something they do most of their waking hours—was what Dad had in mind.)

My wife, Mary, quickly learned the key to a good rapport with my mother. During her first meal at Mom's house, she asked for second helpings. Mom eagerly complied, saying that now she was sure Mary liked her cooking because, she reasoned, Mary might eat the first helping to be polite but would only ask for seconds if she really liked it. After that, Mary asked for seconds on just about everything.

Mom, who died at age 99 in 2013, didn't look like the stereotypical Italian mother. She didn't wear black, though my father had been dead since 1966. She didn't have a mole on her cheek or wear her hair in a bun. And she wasn't under five feet tall. However, she did exhibit those motherly qualities that we have all come to know, love, and occasionally discuss with our therapists. For Mom, the family was everything. When it came to our well-being, she exhibited warmth, tenderness, an iron will, and incredible stamina. She sought out every bargain imaginable but never at the expense of quality.

I still marvel at how she handled the family budget. She'd shop at three or four supermarkets to get the best buys. Occasionally, I'd go with her. "You see this?" she'd say to me, holding a can of corn. "At the Acme this is 49 cents, here it's 39 cents, and across the street it's 59 cents." And so it went with every item. Calculators? Are you kidding? Mom was married for twenty years before she even got a checking account.

And when it came to coupons, Mom was a virtuoso. In those days, some supermarkets didn't just deduct the amount of the coupon from the bill. Customers received cash for manufacturers' coupons, whether or not they purchased those products—as long as the supermarket carried the product. I can still see Mom with her wad of coupons, getting paid by the cashier, and I'd think, *I'm almost sure Mom just made a profit at this supermarket.* If Mom ran the Pentagon, there would never be such a thing as cost overruns. ("You paid how much for ground beef?") In fact, the Defense Department would have a surplus every year.

Mom is an alumna of several schools of feeding and eating. One is the "Always Cook Twice as Much as You Need Because You Never Know Who's Going to Drop By" school. Since it was well known among neighbors and relatives that Mom graduated from this school with honors (magna cum sugo), we probably had more visitors at dinnertime than most other people.

"Oh, I'm sorry, you're eating dinner. I'll come back later."

"No, no, no. Have a seat. Let me give you a small plate of spaghetti with meatballs, braciola, and spareribs. Would you like a beer?"

My uncle Charlie used to stop by frequently for a snack on his way home to dinner. Uncle Charlie married a non-Italian (sometimes called an American but pronounced "MeriCAHN," sometimes with a mildly derisive tone). His wife, Aunt Betty, was a wonderful woman with a mild and charming southern accent. She was also a good cook, but you know how finicky those Italians are about their sauce.

We always called it "sauce," by the way, not "gravy," the way they do in Philadelphia, where I live. When I was a freshman at the University of Pennsylvania, my roommate, Joe Armao, who was from the Philadelphia suburbs (and whose father grew up in South Philly) was talking about gravy and pasta one day. I thought, *People in Philly are weird. Gravy in Buffalo—and probably everywhere else—is the brown stuff you put on mashed potatoes or turkey. These guys are putting it on pasta.* Then Joe went into detail about the gravy, and I realized it was the same kind of sauce Mom made.

My younger brother, Russ, continued Uncle Charlie's tradition until Mom died, even after Russ had been married for decades. Though he lived in the suburbs for many years, he would still stop by a few times a week. He knew that Mom was always in a state of food readiness. He also knew that his wife, Jill (another MeriCAHN), never got any closer to making Mom's sauce than opening a can of tomato soup.

It was quite a tight squeeze every night at the kitchen table. Oh, we had a dining room, but that was reserved for special occasions, like holidays and wakes. Mainly, the dining room was something you passed through to get from the living room to the kitchen.

The kitchen was not only the geographic center of the house but the focal point of our lives. Someone was always in the kitchen, preparing food, eating, or cleaning up. The kitchen had direct access to the side entrance, through which everyone came, unless it was someone formal, like our insurance man, who stopped by once or twice a year to collect his premium and indicate it was paid in his book, which was about the size of the collected works of Shakespeare. Even if you did come in via the front door, you at least had a cup of coffee and some cookies before leaving. Or a glass of schnapps. (More on schnapps later.)

We ate a lot, and that meant Mom was usually cooking something. She was always receptive to trying new dishes, though her regular repertoire would be considered exotic by most standards. Her motto was, "You never know if you're going to like something until you try it." This was usually followed by the story of how she hated beets until she tried them and, of course, liked them.

Though Russ grew to love just about everything Mom cooked, as a kid he had difficulty accepting some of the more exotic dishes on Mom's menu, like cardoons, the slightly bitter thistle related to the artichoke. After myriad stall tactics and piercing stares from my father (along with threats to be locked in the basement and fed only raw onions), he would chew, but never swallow, the offending food. Then, he would feign illness or ask to go to the bathroom. Miraculously, upon his return, the food was gone.

Russ was the comedian of the dining table. It was like getting a floor show every night. I think it was a way of taking his mind off the weird food he was forced to eat. You see, Russ was really a peanut-butter-and-jelly guy trapped in a family that lusted for braciola and cardoons. I never thought to ask Mom, but it now occurs to me that maybe he was left on our doorstep by some Anglo-Saxon family who thought he would never go hungry at our house.

Looking back, I now realize that Russ was ahead of his time with those antics at supper. Unbeknownst to all of us, we were witnessing early dinner theater. Unfortunately, Dad was not amused. Since he believed eating was serious business, he wanted virtual silence at all meals. Thus, Russ often took his life in his hands when he upset the serenity and burst into a routine. Dad wasn't the only one who was unnerved. Once Russ made my older brother, Frank, laugh so hard the meatball he was eating went through his nose. After that incident, I always ate in quick bites so as not to choke to death from Russ's next round of slapstick mortar fire. To this day, I still eat faster than good digestion warrants, somehow subconsciously thinking Russ is going to pop up and make me gag on an artichoke leaf.

Mom was also a great believer in cleaning your plate. Along with millions of other American kids, we did our part for the starving of China. We, however, always started with more food than other kids did. Cleaning the plate meant eating enough food for an entire Chinese village.

To Mom, if you were eating, you were healthy. If you were not eating, you were sick or dead. Every time I'd tell my mother that I was trying to lose a few pounds, she'd take on a worried air, as if I had told her I started using heroin for recreational purposes. "Oh, no, Sam, don't lose any more weight, you're too thin already."

Diets were vague ordeals that we heard went on in suburban neighborhoods, where people played tennis, drove Ford Country Squire station wagons, and ate things like watercress and yogurt. To Mom, the denial of food to anyone was cruel and unusual punishment. On those rare occasions when a guest—usually a non-Italian—would say they weren't hungry, Mom's instant response was "Eat! You'll get hungry."

Though it seemed a little odd at the time, now that I think of it, Mom's command made sense. It was like having an hors d'oeuvre or an *aperitivo*. A nibble here, a sip there, and—presto!—you're hungry.

We ate pasta twice a week because Dad wanted it. Dad had few demands—that we go to church together on Sunday at the 11:30 mass; that we never take a called third strike in baseball; that dinner be ready within moments of his arrival from work (signaled by the jingling of his keys in the door) at 5:15 p.m.; and that we eat pasta twice a week.

Pasta was never referred to as pasta. It was spaghetti or macaroni or lasagna. Pasta is what people who never ate it twice a week call it today because pasta is chic, and they buy exotic pastas made from buckwheat or beets. Mom made sauce once a week. That was good for two meals. The pot Mom used for the sauce was approximately the size of a hot tub. My wife, Mary, asked me what we did with leftover sauce from the second day. With what I'm sure was a strange look on my face, I said, "We didn't have any."

The pasta we used, though not nearly as eclectic as today's shapes, was still varied enough from the standard spaghetti. One of my favorites was something we called "stove-pipes." It was cylindrically shaped macaroni about one-quarter inch in diameter, two inches in length, and cut diagonally at each end. In those days, it was called mostaccioli.

Today, we know it as penne. (Italians often give different names to the same shape of pasta due to regional preferences and dialects.)

There is another pasta we ate less often called bucatini (also known as perciatelli). It was a thick spaghetti about the diameter of a drinking straw, but longer. It was too long to put straight into your mouth and not pliable enough to twirl with your fork. Consequently, you always made a mess by stabbing and cutting it and getting sauce all over the place. Not surprisingly, this was Russ's favorite pasta.

Lasagna was our holiday pasta because it took longer to make. Everybody loved Mom's lasagna except Uncle Alphonso, who refused to eat it because it contained cheese. More on Uncle Alphonso later.

The following are Mom's recipes for spaghetti sauce with meats and lasagna. She always seemed to have some on hand, no matter when we stopped by. It never failed to satisfy, even when we were not hungry.

The Guginos with aunts, uncles, cousins, and Grandma at a holiday dinner

MOM'S SAUCE

For the Hocks and Ribs

2 fresh ham hocks

1 slab (about 2 1/2 pounds)
   of spareribs (St. Louis style,
   not baby back ribs)

For the Sauce

3 tablespoons olive oil

1 large onion, finely chopped,
   about 1 1/2 cups

3 cloves garlic, finely chopped

2 (28-ounce) cans tomato
   puree

2 (12-ounce) cans tomato
   paste

1–2 tablespoons chopped
   fresh basil

1–2 teaspoons oregano*

1–2 bay leaves

2 tablespoons freshly grated
   Romano cheese*

Salt and pepper to taste

For the Meatballs

2 slices Italian bread or
   quality white bread, each
   about 1/2-inch thick (about
   4 ounces), crusts removed

1 1/2 cups warm water

1 pound ground chuck

3 eggs

1 tablespoon freshly grated
   Romano cheese

1 tablespoon chopped parsley

1 tablespoon chopped fresh
   mint

Salt and pepper to taste*

1/4 cup olive oil or canola oil

Pasta

6 quarts of water

1 tablespoon salt

2 pounds of your favorite
   dried pasta

For the Braciola

1 round steak, about 1 pound,
   butterflied and pounded
   thin (about 10 x 6 inches)

Fat trimmed from the
   spareribs

4 tablespoons meatball
   mixture

2 hard-boiled eggs, sliced
   widthwise

1 small onion, minced, about
   1/2 cup

1 tablespoon chopped parsley

1 teaspoon chopped fresh
   mint

1 tablespoon grated Romano
   cheese*

1/4 cup olive oil or canola oil

For the Table

2 cups (or more) grated
   Romano cheese

8–10 leaves of fresh basil

1. Put the hocks in a medium to large saucepan. Cover with water and bring to a boil. Reduce heat and simmer for 1 hour or until they just begin to get tender. Drain, pat dry, and set aside. Meanwhile, trim any excess fat from the ribs, saving the trimmings for braciola. Cut the ribs into individual portions and set aside.

2. Put a heavy kettle—large enough to hold the sauce and meat—over medium heat. Add the oil, and sauté the onion lightly for a few minutes. Add the garlic. Stir frequently (and lower the heat, if needed) to avoid burning.

3. When the onions are soft but not brown, add the puree and paste. Rinse out any remnants from the puree and paste cans with three puree cans full of water and add that water to the pot. Add the remaining sauce ingredients and bring to a simmer, stirring periodically. The sauce will simmer a total of three hours.

4. Just before the hocks are finished cooking on the stove, heat the oven to 450 degrees.

5. Season the hocks and ribs with salt and pepper. Place on a rack over a sheet pan and bake in the oven until browned, about 20 to 25 minutes. Add the hocks and ribs to the sauce.

6. For the meatballs, dip the bread in water, squeeze dry, and crumble with your fingers or chop. (The pieces don't have to be uniform, but none should be too big.) Put the bread and the remaining ingredients for the meatballs, except the oil, in a bowl and mix well. Set aside 4 tablespoons of the meatball mixture for the braciola.

7. Lay the flattened round steak on a work surface and season with salt and pepper. Spread the reserved sparerib trimmings over the steak. Add the reserved meatball mixture and the remaining ingredients, with eggs last. Keep the stuffing away from the edges. Roll lengthwise, tuck in the ends, then continue rolling until you have a very thick "cigar." Tie with string. Secure with skewers if necessary. (You can also wrap the braciola with cheesecloth if you're having problems plugging holes in the steak.)

8. Put a large cast-iron or similar skillet over medium heat. Add the olive oil or canola oil. When the oil is hot, add the braciola. Brown on all sides, and add to the sauce. (Or, you can bake the braciola as you did the ribs and hocks.)

9. Form meatballs about 1 1/2 inches in diameter. Put the skillet used for the braciola over medium heat. Add the olive or canola oil. When hot but not smoking, add the meatballs and fry until well browned on all sides. Drain on paper towels and set aside.

10. After the sauce has simmered 2 1/2 hours, add the meatballs. Cook an additional 1/2 hour. Stir gently to avoid breaking the meatballs.

11. Bring 6 quarts of water to a rolling boil in a large pot. Add the salt and pasta. Cook according to package instructions, tasting it to make sure it is done to your taste. (Ideally, it should be al dente, tender but still firm.) Drain the pasta in a large colander. Return it to the cooking pot and toss it with a cup or two of the sauce to coat. Cover and keep warm while you arrange the meat.

12. Remove the meatballs to a large shallow bowl. Put the spareribs and hocks on a platter. Remove the string and skewers from the braciola (and cheesecloth, if using). Cut into 3/4-inch-thick slices and add to the ribs and hocks.

13. Serve the pasta with additional sauce, grated cheese, and basil, which is torn or cut with a paring knife over the pasta.

Serves 8 Italians or 10 or more non-Italians.

* See "Pantry" (page 164) at the end of the book for information on salt, pepper, tomatoes, oregano, Romano cheese, and pasta.

MOM'S LASAGNA

Mom always made enough sauce for two meals, usually for two meals with spaghetti or macaroni. For holidays, a double recipe would be entirely devoted to lasagna. The variation in lasagna sheets is because not all lasagna pans are created equal. The one I used was 13 inches long, 9 inches wide, and 3 inches deep and took 24 noodles, six for each of the four layers.

20–24 lasagna noodles, depending on your pan (There are typically 20 noodles in a pound.)

1 tablespoon of salt

1 cup plus 1 quart spaghetti sauce, plus additional for the table (See previous Mom's Sauce recipe.)

2 pounds whole-milk or part-skim ricotta

1 1/2 pounds cooked meatballs, crushed*

1 cup freshly grated Romano cheese, plus additional for the table

5 eggs, beaten with a pinch of salt

1. Bring at least four quarts of water to a rolling boil. Add 1 tablespoon of salt and half the lasagna noodles. Cook according to package instructions. Remove the noodles with tongs and lay them on clean kitchen towels to cool. Repeat with the remaining noodles. The noodles should be a bit short of al dente. (If you have a very large pot, you can do all the noodles at one time.)

2. Heat the oven to 350 degrees.

3. Spread half of the 1 cup of sauce in a thin layer on the bottom of a glass or enamel baking pan approximately 13 x 9 x 3 inches. (The other 1/2 cup will cover the top of the finished lasagna.) Cover the bottom of the pan lengthwise with five of the lasagna noodles. If the noodles don't cover the length of the pan, place one noodle widthwise over the uncovered space. Use only whole sheets. Broken pieces can be used in the middle of the lasagna.

4. Add the remaining ingredients in the following order: 1/3 each of the ricotta, crushed meatballs, grated cheese, sauce (from the 1 quart), and the beaten eggs. Cover with the second layer of noodles. Then repeat the process with the remaining filling and noodles until you have four layers of noodles and three layers of filling. The top layer should be noodles topped with the remaining 1/2 cup of sauce.

5. Cover with foil and bake for 35–40 minutes or until the internal temperature of the lasagna is 165 degrees. Let rest for 1/2 hour before serving. Serve with additional sauce and grated cheese.

* Mom's sauce recipe makes about 1 pound of cooked meatballs, so I suggest doubling the recipe for the meatballs. Use 1 1/2 pounds of it in the lasagna and put the remaining meatballs in the sauce with the other meats.

MOM'S VARIATION ON GRANDMA'S BAKED MACARONI

Just as I occasionally tweak Mom's recipes, Mom did the same with Grandma's baked macaroni.

Grandma's recipe had three eggs instead of six. And you just scooped it out of the pan rather than inverting it onto a platter. This could be a good use for the second day of Mom's Sauce if you have enough left over. You could even use any leftover meatballs in place of some of the ground beef.

4 quarts water

1 tablespoon salt

1 pound ziti

1 pound ground chuck

Salt and pepper to taste

1 1/2 quarts (6 cups) Mom's Sauce

1 tablespoon olive oil or olive oil spray

1 cup grated Romano cheese, plus more for topping (optional) and for the table

6 eggs, beaten

* The dimensions for the pan are not set in stone. Just make sure it's big enough (at least 240 square inches) and deep enough (not less than 2 inches) to hold the ingredients.

1. Cook the ziti in four quarts of boiling water with 1 tablespoon of salt for a minute or two less than called for in the package instructions. It should still be quite firm.

2. While the ziti is cooking, brown the ground chuck in a large skillet. Drain off any excess fat. Season with salt and pepper. Add 2 cups of spaghetti sauce. Stir well, bring to a simmer, and cook for 5 minutes. Set aside.

3. While the sauce simmers, heat the oven to 350 degrees.

4. Drain the cooked ziti and combine with the meat sauce.

5. Brush or spray the oil on the bottom and sides of a baking pan approximately 9 x 13 x 3 inches.* Combine the 1 cup of cheese with the eggs. Season with salt and pepper to taste. Pour 1/3 of egg and cheese mixture on the bottom of the baking pan. Put the pan in the oven until the mixture just begins to set, about 5–6 minutes.

6. Put half of the ziti/meat mixture in the baking pan and spread evenly. Spread half of the remaining egg/cheese mixture evenly over the ziti/meat mixture. Add 3/4 cup of the reserved sauce. Repeat with the rest of the macaroni/meat mixture, the egg/cheese mixture, and 3/4 cup sauce. Add a little more sauce if the top isn't well covered. Top with more cheese, if desired.

7. Cover with foil and bake for 35 minutes.

8. Remove the macaroni from the oven and let stand 15 to 20 minutes.

9. Meanwhile, heat the remaining sauce.

10. Invert the baked macaroni onto a platter. Cut the macaroni into 6 to 8 pieces. Serve with the additional sauce and grated cheese. Serves 6 to 8.

CAN DO

A neighbor of ours once said, "If there's ever a nuclear war, I know exactly where to go—your mother's basement." She said this because she knew what my mother kept down there—everything.

Essentially, what Mom had in her basement was a flea market waiting to be discovered. To my knowledge, Mom never threw anything away, except for things like banana peels and corn husks. The refrigerator we brought with us from the old neighborhood decades before, the one with the freezer compartment you had to wedge shut with a piece of cardboard, was there. Also, plates, platters, silverware, glasses, bowls, furniture, old overcoats, shoes, sneakers, galoshes, small appliances that no longer worked, and tools that worked but were no longer used. There was wrapping paper from every gift she ever received, clear plastic containers from take-out joints, coffee cans, those rectangular Styrofoam plates that come under the meat you buy in supermarkets, and shopping bags from stores that had long since gone out of business. There were things we wore and played with as kids, including the rug I slept on in kindergarten, a globe she bought to help us learn geography, a jacket I received as a member of a championship high school football team, and washcloths that were once a terry-cloth robe I took to college.

But the most important reason for seeking refuge from the holocaust in Mom's basement was food. The refrigerator was always fully stocked with a variety of food, which may have included spaghetti sauce, roasted meats such as ham, turkey, or beef, homemade pies, vegetables, and assorted beverages. A separate chest freezer had all our favorites—tripe, *billulata* (a kind of stromboli), homemade sausage and meatballs, as well as numerous supermarket specials that Mom bought by the gross.

The floor was littered with partially filled cases of beer, soda ("pop" in our neck of the woods), mixers, and wine. We were never big wine drinkers. Most of the wine was in half bottles with twist-off caps that Mom got as door prizes at canasta parties.

The crowning jewel of Mom's food stockpile was what we called the fruit cellar. Its name is derived from a time when basements were no more than dug-out caves to store food for the winter. In our case, it was really an indoor shed built by my father to house all of Mom's canning. Dad built it the first year we moved in. Several years later, he built a water closet in the basement, which gives you an idea of our priorities.

Mom's canning wasn't a hobby. There was nothing dainty about it. You wouldn't see any cute little jars with frilly stickers that read "rhubarb marmalade" or "pickled watermelon rind." These products were not intended for Christmas Pollyanna gifts. This was the result of a no-nonsense, assembly-line, knock-'em-out production.

We're talking necessities of life here. This was food for the winter and maybe into next summer, if you were lucky. This was sustenance for four male behemoths and a daughter who was no slouch either. This was also for people who dropped by more often than we could count, most of whom knew the gustatorial value of what was contained in those jars and weren't too embarrassed to ask for it.

When Mom's canning factory was at its zenith, she was turning out 500 quarts or more of tomatoes, 110 or more quarts each of pears and peaches, 50 or so jars of Concord grape jam (we had an arbor in the backyard that my father planted soon after we moved in), and smaller amounts of eggplant, cardoons, and strawberry and raspberry jams.

People wondered why my mother's tomato sauces were so good. Well, when you feed it to your family two to three times a week on everything from pizza to pasta to snails, it's got to be good. And when you can perfectly ripe, locally grown tomatoes, you have half of the battle won.

If I had to pick one identifying symbol of the canning season, it would be the appearance of Bartlett pears, the perfume of which was, for me, more intoxicating than any cologne. The fact that the Bartlett pear season was so short (in Buffalo, at least) made them all the more dear. Fortunately, Mom was able to capture and preserve the special quality of those pears so that we could enjoy them year-round.

Mom's canned peaches were the most popular. They were so good, I never had a strong urge to eat fresh ones. (I didn't like the fuzz anyway.) You could always tell Mom's peaches from anyone else's. Hers were the ones with the peach pit at the bottom of the jar. When I asked Mom why she left the pit in the jar, she said, "You know, a lot of people have asked me that. I'm not sure why or what it does, exactly, except that somehow it seems to give an 'essence' to the fruit. Anyway, people tell me they've never tasted peaches as good."

Canning started as early as May with cardoons, a thistle related to artichokes with a bitter, acquired taste. Strawberries and raspberries came in June and July. However, the significant canning did not begin until late August. I remember that time very well. We were all getting ready for school. Preseason pro football—which my father mockingly called "exhibition" football—was underway. And in Buffalo, it was time to start thinking about snow tires and storm windows.

The canning was done in the basement. Everything needed was there—sinks, a stove, tables, plenty of room. A lot of Italians used their basements for everyday cooking so they wouldn't spoil their "nice" kitchen upstairs. One family on the block also ate in the basement unless they had company.

There were specific requirements for the operation. Mom used only local, ripe tomatoes, though not the Roma or plum tomatoes one associates with Italian cooking. When I asked Mom why, she just shrugged and said, "Because I never used them." (A quintessential Mom answer, akin to today's "It is what it is.")

The peaches were a kind of freestone (meaning the pit comes away easily from the flesh) called Hale Haven. If Hale Havens weren't available, she used Alberta peaches.

All the food was packed in glass jars, mostly quart size. Early on, Mom used those blue-tinted Mason jars with glass tops, fastened by a metal-hinged snap. As the years passed, she used the more conventional screw-top jars. And those blue-tinted jars found their way into antique shops and flea markets.

The canned goods were boiled in a large, dark-blue-with-white-specks enamel pot, the kind you might see at a clam bake. A wire insert held about six jars and kept them from rolling about.

The entire process was done by hand. No Cuisinarts here. Just Mom, my aunt Sandy, Grandma, and a lot of sweat. (We called grandma Nana, pronounced NAH-nah, the Sicilian dialect for nonna, the traditional Italian name for grandmother.)

The most exotic tool they used was a paring knife. Mom would peel the fruit with the knife, using her thumb as a strike plate. With each movement, the blade would bang against her thumb. Eventually, Mom's thumb began to look more like a big toe, nicely calloused and virtually impervious to pain.

Some things changed over the years. The most dramatic was the cost of food. Mom used to buy tomatoes for $1 a bushel and peaches for $3. After Grandma died and Aunt Sandy became ill, canning became a one-person operation. Mom still canned into her 80s but at a much slower pace.

Because we ate so much good food, we never worried about nutrition as such. But as she got older, Mom paid more attention to her diet, which explains another change. She cut in half the amount of sugar she used in the canned peaches and pears.

Even when Mom's canning production shrank—and eventually stopped when she was 83—we were hardly around enough to eat it. "I wish you kids would take more food with you," she said as she tried to stuff another jar of tomatoes into my suitcase. This virtually precluded using a carry-on bag. Mom never understood that. She thought a plane was just a big car that flew. Once, when she came to visit my brother in Washington, DC, she brought a complete spaghetti dinner for ten people on the plane with her.

I would sometimes get carried away with the canned food I brought back with me from Buffalo. Eating an entire jar of peaches at a sitting was not uncommon. Even that might not be enough sometimes. Then I might suck on a peach pit, hoping it would pacify me until the urge subsided. I'd be fine until I happened to see a preseason (OK, Dad, "exhibition") football game on television or passed a fruit stand selling Bartlett pears.

Canned jars of tomatoes, pears, eggplant, and caponata, just the way Mom did them

TO BOIL OR NOT TO BOIL, THAT IS THE QUESTION

You will notice that in the following recipes the canned tomatoes and pears are boiled but the eggplant is not. (Ditto for the canned peaches and caponata in the Can II chapter.) Why? The short answer is: That's the way Mom did it. The more formal answer is that while everything you canned in years past had to be boiled, in recent years more and more information on canning, including from the US Department of Agriculture, suggests boiling is not needed *if the jars are sterilized and properly sealed*. That said, if you aren't sure you followed proper procedures or you just want to play it safe, boil the canned eggplant and caponata in the same way the tomatoes were boiled. Whether you do or don't, before consuming home-canned foods, check to see that:

- The jar lid is firmly sealed and concave.
- Nothing has leaked from the jar.
- No liquid spurts out when the jar is opened.
- No unnatural or "off" odors can be detected.

RINGS AND LIDS

You don't need to sterilize lids or rings. In fact, boiling the lids may prevent them from making a proper seal. However, you should buy new lids each time you can. Rings can be reused as long as they are not dented or rusted. Just make sure they're clean.

CANNED TOMATOES

Mom used the round, locally grown, everyday-eating tomatoes, the kind you'd put in a salad or on a sandwich. In summer, these are often called "field tomatoes" to distinguish them from the more expensive heirloom tomatoes, which I wouldn't use in this recipe. But you might consider using the oblong Roma tomatoes, which have thicker skins and fewer seeds. In addition to a pot large enough to hold the jars, you'll need a rack that fits inside the pot. Normally this holds six quarts, which is handy if you want to double the recipe.

3 (1-quart) jars with lids and rings (also called bands)

7 to 8 pounds ripe but still somewhat firm locally grown tomatoes

6 large fresh basil leaves
Salt

1. Sterilize the jars by putting them in a pot large enough to cover the jars with 1 to 2 inches of water. Stabilize the jars with a wire rack that fits inside a large kettle. Bring the water to a temperature of 180 degrees for 10 minutes. Turn off the heat. You can leave the jars in the hot water up to an hour before filling them. When ready to fill, carefully pour the water out of each jar back into the pot, and put each jar upside down on a clean cloth.

2. Meanwhile, bring a 3- to 4-quart pot of water to a simmer and fill a bowl or tub with ice water. In batches, blanch the tomatoes in the simmering water for 1 to 2 minutes. Drop them into the ice water. After a minute or two, peel and core them and set them aside in a bowl.

3. Put two basil leaves in the bottom of each sterilized jar. Pack the jars halfway with tomatoes. Add a scant teaspoon of salt to each jar. Add the remaining tomatoes, pressing them down with a wooden spoon. If the tomatoes are too large, cut them in half or quarters. Tomatoes should reach up to 1/2 inch from the top of the jar.

4. Wipe the tops of the jars with a clean cloth. Put on the lid, and secure with the ring. Seal snugly but not tightly by hand.

5. Put the jars into the same pot used to sterilize the jars, secured with a wire insert. Make sure the jars are covered with water, as they were when sterilized. Bring the water to a boil. Boil gently for 10 minutes.

6. Turn off the heat and carefully remove the jars from the pot. (Ball, the manufacturer of canning jars, suggests leaving the jars in the water with the heat turned off for 5 minutes. I can't recall if Mom did that, but it can't hurt.) Seal the jars tightly. Let cool for 48 hours. Store in a cool place like a cellar. Makes 3 quarts.

CANNED PEARS

3 (1-quart) canning jars with lids and rings

3 cups sugar

4 1/2 cups water

5–6 pounds Bartlett pears

1. See "Canned Tomatoes" recipe for sterilizing instructions.

2. While the canning jars are being sterilized, combine the sugar and water in a saucepan. Bring to a simmer, stirring with a wooden spoon just until the sugar dissolves and the liquid becomes clear. Set aside.

3. Peel and core pears. Cut them in half lengthwise, and put them in cold water until you're ready to pack them.

4. Pack the pear halves in each of the sterilized canning jars with the hollowed-out core part down. (About 7 or 8 halves per jar, depending on size.) Overlap the pear halves until you reach 1/2 inch from the top of the jar. Drain off any juice. Pour in the syrup until it reaches 1/4 inch from the top of the jar.

5. Wipe the tops of the jars with a clean kitchen towel. Put on the lid, and secure with the ring. Seal snugly but not tightly by hand. Put the jars in the same pot used to sterilize the jars, secured with a wire insert. Make sure the jars are covered with water, as they were when sterilized.

6. Bring the water to a boil. Boil for 15 minutes. Remove the jars and seal tightly. Let cool for 48 hours. Store in a cool place like a cellar. Makes 3 quarts.

PICKLED EGGPLANT

Mom used "wide mouth" jars (3 1/4 inches wide) for pickled eggplant because the eggplant slices wouldn't fit in the opening of the more standard jar mouth, which is 2 1/2 inches wide.

3 (1-quart) wide-mouth canning jars with lids and rings

6 medium eggplants, about 6 pounds

Salt

1 1/2 quarts red wine vinegar

4 to 4 1/2 cups olive oil

3 cloves garlic, peeled and cut into slivers

Red pepper flakes

Oregano

1. Sterilize jars as above.

2. Trim the ends and peel each eggplant. Cut into 1/2-inch-thick round slices. Salt the slices on both sides, and place in a colander (not overlapping) for at least 1 hour. (If all the eggplant will not fit in one colander, do this step in batches. You could also employ a cake rack.)

3. Bring the vinegar to a boil in a pot wide enough to hold 4 or 5 slices of eggplant at one time. Pat the eggplant slices dry with paper towels. Cook the slices in batches in the vinegar, each batch for about 5 minutes or until the eggplant is soft but not mushy. Turn the slices over halfway through cooking. Remove eggplant to platters or sheet pans lined with paper towels to cool.

4. Pour some of the olive oil into a bowl or soup plate. Dip the eggplant slices in the oil, then stack them inside each of the canning jars. Season every other layer with a sliver of garlic, a pinch of red pepper flakes, and a pinch of oregano.

5. Fill each jar to 1/2 inch from the top. Add the remaining oil to each jar until all slices are covered. Seal the jars tightly. Makes 3 quarts.

WEEDING OUT A DELICIOUS GREEN

Are you familiar with the expression about lighting a candle rather than cursing the darkness? Think of that proverb as you gaze at your weed-covered lawn this spring. No, I'm not suggesting that you set fire to your weeds. Instead, eat them.

Dandelions, which sound less menacing than weeds, are delicious greens when used raw in salads or cooked and eaten, as you would spinach. When I was a kid, eating greens like dandelions, especially if they came from the front lawn, was about as appetizing for non-Italians as tripe. But in recent years, hearty or bitter greens like collards, and especially kale, have become quite popular.

Dandelions have been around for quite a while, even before the first housewife interrupted her husband's Sunday afternoon nap to remind him to weed the lawn. For many years, before Mr. Birdseye figured out how to give us broccoli year-round, people looked forward to spring and the coming of verdant dandelions after enduring long winters in which the only vegetables they ate were brown.

Mom weeded the front lawn each spring for her supply of dandelions. She used this old, rusty knife with a worn wooden handle that was falling apart. It looked like a relic from a museum exhibit featuring primitive tools of the Bronze Age. (See photo, page 31.)

The name *dandelion* is derived from the French *dent de lion*—literally, tooth of the lion—so called because of the jagged outline of the leaves. At home, we called dandelion "*cicordia*," thinking it was a member of the chicory family. (The correct Italian spelling is "*cicoria*.") Close, but no cigar. Dandelion and chicory both belong to the large Compositae family, but each is in a different genus within that family, according to *The Oxford Companion to Food* by Alan Davidson (Oxford University Press).

The French and the rest of Europe, like Mom, prefer dandelions in their wild state. (When I was in Greece, the farmers' markets were loaded with what Greeks call *horta*, the term for wild greens, including dandelion.) American agribusiness, however, has developed several strains of dandelion that can be grown all year. Beginning in midwinter, large-leaf and toothless dandelions—an indication that domesticity has removed some of their bite—from California, Texas, and Florida become available.

As spring breaks, the more traditional type, like the ones on your lawn, begins to appear. Years ago, that meant sometime in mid-April or so. But with climate change, dandelions can start to flower by the end of March. Mom always picked the dandelions before they flowered, thinking that the flowers weren't edible, though apparently, they are (along with the roots), according to *The Oxford Companion to Food*. Later in spring and into early summer, local cultivated varieties start showing up.

Give me the stuff from the lawn any day. Its delicate texture belies its flavorful and pleasant bitterness. My guess is it's also more nutritious than the mass-produced stuff, though I can't prove it. Both types, however, are very healthful. Dandelions have huge amounts of vitamin A and are high in vitamin C, iron, potassium, calcium, and fiber. We didn't know about that as kids, though Mom always said dandelions were "loaded with vitamins." Mom also told us that the cooking water from dandelions (known as the *pot liquor* to old-fashioned Southern cooks who boiled their greens for hours) was good for us. So, we drank it. Not as tasty as Mom's chicken soup but a lot better than the cod liver oil she made us take when we were young. (Dandelions are also known for their diuretic properties, which is why the other French name for them is *pissenlit*, "pissabed" in English.)

My family, like most Italian families, ate dandelions with very little adornment. They were boiled and dressed only with oil, salt, pepper, and garlic. But Mom also used the greens in an omelet (what we'd call a frittata today) on meatless Fridays and during Lent. These were round omelets, unlike French omelets, which are folded over into half-moons.

Dandelions that are fresh and free from bruises make wonderful salads, prepared in much the same way you'd fix a spinach salad, with chopped hard-cooked eggs and a warm bacon-vinegar dressing. Dandelions go well with roasted meats and make a delicious stuffing ingredient for breast of lamb or veal.

Many people eat dandelions and other greens with some kind of pork. While Black folks may combine their greens (typically collards or kale) with smoked ham hocks, Italians are more likely to eat them with sausage. In Philadelphia, my home since graduating from college in 1970 (with an 11-year hiatus in California and New York from 1989 to 2000), there used to be a great little hangout for South Philly politicos called Shank's, a block away from the Ninth Street Italian Market. There, Shank and his wife Evelyn kept a pile of cooked greens (dandelion in season or broccoli di rape). And while a cigarette dangled from her lips, Evelyn served them with Italian sausage or sliced roast pork on what we in Philly call a hoagie or a steak (as in cheesesteak) roll. It's the same type of bread used for heroes, subs, and grinders elsewhere in the country. However, everyone in Philly knows that the quality of a hoagie or cheesesteak is at least half dependent on the quality of the bread. As to whether the sausage or pork canceled out the nutrition in the greens, I wouldn't have dared to broach the subject at Shank's. Evelyn might have put out her cigarette in my hoagie.

From bottom, clockwise: Mom's meat grinder, all-purpose kitchen knife, dandelion and cardoon cutter. Also, an ashtray and letter opener Dad made in World War II from bullets and shells.

DANDELION GREENS WITH GARLIC AND OLIVE OIL

When I was writing *Low-Fat Cooking to Beat the Clock* (Chronicle), I learned the secret of cooking garlic in the water used to cook greens instead of cooking the garlic in olive oil. Once the garlic is cooked in that water and tossed with the greens, smaller amounts of higher-quality olive oil are added. This allows more olive oil flavor to come through, despite using less of it. This recipe originally had twice as much oil.

2 teaspoons salt plus more to taste

2 pounds dandelion greens

2–3 cloves garlic, finely chopped

2 tablespoons high-quality extra-virgin olive oil

Pepper to taste

Red pepper flakes (optional)

1. Bring 4 quarts of water to a boil. Stir in 2 teaspoons of salt when the water reaches a boil.

2. Meanwhile, if using wild dandelions, cut off their roots. Remove any tough or dried-out stems, and remove any bruised or slimy leaves. If the dandelions are in good-sized bunches, like most cultivated ones, cut the bunches in half, crosswise. Clean the dandelions in a tub of cool water and drain in a colander. (Wild dandelions, the ones you pick from your lawn, as Mom did, may need two changes of water to remove all the grit.)

3. Add the cleaned and drained dandelions to the boiling salted water. Stir, cover, and return to a boil. Uncover and cook for 5 minutes or until just tender. Smaller, more-delicate wild dandelions will take less time. In any case, try to keep them relatively firm. Drain the dandelions in a colander, leaving a cup of the cooking water in the pot. Squeeze out excess moisture from the dandelions with the back of a large spoon or ladle.

4. Add the garlic to the pot and cook over medium heat for 2 minutes. Return the dandelions to the pot. Add the olive oil and salt and pepper, and red pepper flakes, if desired. Turn off the heat and mix thoroughly but gently for a few minutes. Serve warm or at room temperature. Serves 4.

DANDELION FRITTATA

2 pounds dandelion greens

Salt and pepper to taste

6 eggs

1/4 cup grated Romano cheese (or a combination of Romano and Parmigiano)

2 tablespoons extra-virgin olive oil

2 cloves garlic, chopped

1. Clean and cook the dandelions as done in steps 1–3 in the above recipe. Chop the dandelions very coarsely and season with salt and pepper.

2. In a bowl large enough to hold the eggs and dandelions, beat the eggs, cheese, salt, and pepper. Add the cooked and drained dandelions, and mix well. Set aside.

3. Turn on the oven broiler. Set a broiling pan or rack 6 to 8 inches from the heat source.

4. Put a 9-inch cast-iron skillet over medium heat. Add the oil. Add the garlic and gently cook until it just turns light brown. Be careful not to burn the garlic.

5. Add the dandelion and egg mixture to the skillet. Cook until the bottom is set and firm. Run a heatproof rubber spatula around the edge of the frittata to make it easier to slip out of the skillet when cooked. When the sides and bottom of the frittata are set, put the skillet under the broiler until the top is firm, a minute or two. Slide the cooked frittata out of the skillet and onto a plate. (You can also serve it directly from the skillet, as I often do.) Serve warm or at room temperature. Serves 2 as an entrée or more when cut into narrow wedges for a buffet table or as part of a tapas spread.

DANDELION AND SAUSAGE HOAGIES

In addition to sausage (see Picnic chapter for Mom's sausage recipe on page 146), you could use leftover roast pork in this recipe. Whichever you use, make sure the roll is top quality.

2 pounds dandelion greens

Salt and pepper to taste

1 pound hot or mild Italian sausage

3 tablespoons olive oil

1–2 cloves garlic, finely chopped (optional)

4 (8-inch-long) hoagie rolls

1. Clean and cook the dandelions, as done in steps 1–3 of the Dandelion Greens recipe. Drain the dandelions, squeeze out excess moisture, chop coarsely, and season to taste with salt and pepper. Set aside.

2. If the sausage is a rope, cut it crosswise into 4 equal pieces. Put them in a frying pan with 1/2 cup of water. Boil the sausages gently, turning a few times, until the water evaporates. Remove the sausages and cut each one in half, lengthwise. Over medium heat, add half the olive oil to the pan. When hot, add the halved sausages, cut side down. Lower the heat. Cook both sides of the sausage until they are lightly brown. Remove the sausages to a platter, and cover to keep warm.

3. Add the remaining oil to the pan over medium heat. If using garlic, cook it for a few minutes, making sure it doesn't burn. Add the greens and cook, tossing, until heated through. Check for seasoning. Put 2 sausage halves on a roll. Top each with 1/4 of the greens. Serves 4.

LENT

One of the advantages of growing up a Catholic is that it provides an enormous amount of material for reminiscence. If you're lucky, you can get away with a minimum of therapy, a livable amount of guilt, and a fair amount of grist for your writing. I prefer the humorous side; it's much less painful.

Which brings us to Lent. The Lent of my youth was one of those bedrock symbols of Catholicism that now seem strange. Looking back on it, it's as if I were reading about the tribal customs of some ancient civilization, like the Incas.

For those unfamiliar, Lent is supposed to commemorate the forty days prior to Jesus's crucifixion, beginning with Ash Wednesday and ending on Easter Sunday. The celebrations preceding, like Mardi Gras in New Orleans and Carnival in Rio de Janeiro, are famous for their excesses because the Lenten period is one of fasting and penance. This is to simulate Jesus's forty-day fast in the desert. For Catholic kids like me, all this ecclesiastical mumbo-jumbo meant just one thing—"giving up" something we liked for Lent.

Giving up something for Lent was like making New Year's resolutions. You didn't really want to do it, but it was supposed to be good for you nevertheless (or so the nuns told us). Of course, it wasn't sufficient to do without something you hated, like beets, brussels sprouts, or liver. No, you had to forego things like cheeseburgers, bubble gum, and Jujyfruits (except the black ones).

The fasting was in addition to the weekly abstinence from meat on Fridays, a tragedy of major proportions in my family. We felt that the Friday sacrifice throughout the year should have given us automatic dispensation from Lent. No such luck. To make matters worse, you were encouraged (but not obliged) to refrain from meat on Wednesdays as well. In my family, this was the equivalent of pounding salt into an open wound. The suffering was supposed to make you a better or perhaps holier human being, something the starving of Africa (and elsewhere) would no doubt be glad to hear. I'm not sure why Wednesday was picked to be the second meatless day rather than, say, Tuesday. Just another one of those Catholic mysteries, I guess.

Within the Lenten period is another special day in my family, St. Joseph's Day. I always felt sorry for poor old St. Joseph. You might say he is the Rodney Dangerfield of saints. He gets no respect. He does have a day named after him, March 19, though I've also seen

March 20. But almost every day in the Catholic calendar has a saint assigned to it. Many of them are unknown to most Catholics, like St. Cyril of Jerusalem (March 18) and St. Nicholas of Flue (March 21), who seems like he should be the patron saint of chimneys.

Here he is, the father of God (or stepfather, if you will) and, unless they're from St. Joseph, Missouri, or go to St. Joseph's University, the only contact most people had with St. Joseph were those tasty orange aspirins that bear his name—the ones I took from the medicine chest when Mom wasn't looking because they tasted like candy. But St. Joseph is a big deal in Sicily, where he is that island's patron saint.

Italians and Catholics, in general, are always praying to some saint. St. Christopher is supposed to watch over travelers, St. Rita is for loneliness, and if you are really in dire straits, St. Jude is the go-to saint for the desperate. Sicilians, like my family, prayed to St. Joseph for, as Mom put it, "favors asked for and favors granted."

According to legend, there was a drought in Sicily during the Middle Ages. The people of Sicily prayed to St. Joseph to end the drought. When their prayers were answered, the people of Sicily prepared a giant feast to which everyone was invited, including the poor. That tradition continues today. (St. Joseph is also the patron saint of the unemployed, which oddly fits in with the many impoverished Sicilians—like my grandparents—who immigrated to America to seek a better life.)

We didn't celebrate St. Joseph's Day every year, only when a specific prayer—and usually a big one at that—was answered. My first St. Joseph celebration took place when I was eight years old. It was in honor of my cousin Therese, the first child of my uncle Alphonso and my aunt Jo, who succeeded in giving birth after years of trying.

As thanks for that granted favor, Mom, Grandma, and Aunt Sandy prepared a St. Joseph's table. It contained enough food to feed three hundred people. The entire spread was meatless because it was Lent. By tradition, there were two grain dishes—rice with lentils and pasta con sarde, pasta with sardines. (Pasta isn't technically a grain, though it is made from a grain. Close enough.) Artichokes, always very popular, were done three ways: sauced, stuffed, and fried. Several varieties of omelets were made, including cauliflower, spinach, and cardoons.

There were fish in the form of fried whiting and sardines. Baccala (dried cod) was reconstituted and baked in tomato sauce. Desserts included cannoli and honey buds (also known as honey balls)—little dough balls rolled in honey and walnuts.

My cousin Therese, now a pediatric cardiologist at Children's Hospital in Philly, told me her family celebrated St. Joseph's Day every year but not with a St. Joseph's table. "We always had pasta con sarde, asparagus frittata, and honey buds," said Therese, who still makes pasta con sarde and tested the recipe in this chapter. Therese's younger brother is named, not surprisingly, Joseph. Like Therese, he's a physician. But Uncle Alphonso wanted him to be a cardinal—the clergyman, not the bird.

The following are some of Mom's recipes for Lent and her St. Joseph's table. Enjoy them, even if you're not giving thanks to St. Joseph or giving up anything for Lent.

ITALIAN-STYLE FRIED CAULIFLOWER

Fresh mint may seem a little surprising in this recipe, but Mom always grew fresh mint (and basil) in two half wine barrels in the backyard. I use panko bread crumbs for this and all breaded foods. Created in Japan but now ubiquitous in the United States, panko has a drier and flakier consistency than regular breadcrumbs and produces lighter and crunchier-tasting fried (or baked) food.

1 head (about 2 pounds) cauliflower

Salt and pepper to taste

2 cups fine bread crumbs

4 tablespoons grated Romano or Parmigiano cheese

2 tablespoons chopped fresh mint

2 teaspoons dried oregano

4 eggs

1 cup olive oil or a neutral oil, like canola oil

1. Cut the cauliflower into florets a bit larger than bite-size. Steam, boil, or microwave the florets until just tender but still firm. Season with salt and pepper. (This can be done hours or the day before and refrigerated. But bring the cauliflower to room temperature before proceeding with the next step.)

2. Combine the bread crumbs, cheese, mint, oregano, salt, and pepper in a pie plate or shallow bowl. Beat the eggs and season with salt and pepper.

3. Dip the cauliflower into the beaten eggs and roll in bread crumb mixture. Put the breaded cauliflower on a cake rack or a sheet pan lined with waxed paper. (This can be done a few hours ahead.)

4. Put a large skillet over medium-high heat. Add the oil. When the oil is hot but not smoking—when a few bread crumbs dropped into it sizzle—add the cauliflower. Cook in batches so as not to crowd the pan. When browned on all sides, drain on paper towels. Serve immediately, or keep warm for a short time in a low oven. Serves 4.

My variation on Mom's pasta con sarde

PASTA CON SARDE

Pasta con sarde is a delightfully exotic dish that I have grown to love. If any dish symbolizes what Sicilians are all about, this is it. Pasta con sarde combines ingredients and influences from all over the Mediterranean—a delicious, if curious, mingling of the cuisines of several countries. More than any other single food, it tells the history of Sicily, one of the most conquered pieces of territory in the world. (Most spellings of this dish are pasta con le sarde. But we never said it that way. In fact, Mom called it something completely different. See below.)

Pasta con sarde also reflects the strong Sicilian commitment to Catholicism. It is traditionally eaten on St. Joseph's Day, which occurs during Lent.

Ironically, I hated pasta con sarde when I was growing up. I'm sure one reason was the Lenten season and the concept of fasting, especially the meatless part. But a more plausible explanation is that the sauce Mom (and many other Sicilians) made was just too heavy.

It's basically a tomato sauce with cauliflower, fennel, and sardines. Pasta con sarde is—or should be—a delicate dish. The tomato sauce, often made with tomato paste and puree, masks that delicacy. Some Sicilian Americans used a canned con sarde sauce, which was dreadful.

In researching recipes for pasta con sarde, I found the absence or sparing use of tomatoes. I also found that no one else except Mom used cauliflower. There is, however, a companion dish to pasta con sarde called *pasta con i broccoli*, which, ironically, uses cauliflower, not broccoli. From Waverly Root's *The Food of Italy* (Atheneum, 1971), I discovered that some recipes call for garnishing the dish with slices of hard-boiled egg. This is peculiar because, although Mom never used it in pasta con sarde, she did make a meatless spaghetti sauce with hard-boiled eggs on Fridays and during Lent. Mom somehow thought that we'd think of the eggs as meatballs. Nice try, Mom.

One final note about the derivations of pasta con sarde. Mom called the pasta con sarde she made with that heavy tomato sauce *pasta alla Milanese*, meaning pasta in the style of Milan. Until I wrote this book, I never considered the obvious contradiction: why is a classic Sicilian dish named after a city at the other end—in every way imaginable—of Italy? It is the equivalent of calling an American dish New York City Gumbo. Mom didn't have an answer, but after a little research, I found out that some Sicilians, who immigrated to Milan, modified the dish—by adding, among other things, tomatoes and tomato paste—and changed its name.

The following recipe is a little of Paula Wolfert, author of *Mediterranean Cooking*, a little of Marcella Hazan, author of *The Classic Italian Cookbook* (which it is), Mom, and me. My cousin Therese, who tested this recipe, said that cleaning the sardines was "not for the weak of heart." And she's a physician! Really, if you've ever cleaned fish, sardines are no different, though because they are small, it's a bit more tedious than cleaning larger fish. Your fishmonger might do it for you, if you'd rather not.

However, if you can't find fresh sardines or would just rather not deal with them, canned sardines are a very good substitute. In fact, after making it with fresh sardines, I used canned sardines on a second test. I found no difference in taste or quality. But the sardines should be of very high quality. In January 2022, *Saveur* magazine listed Jose Gourmet and Matiz Gallego as its top canned sardines. King Oscar, Wild Planet, and Crown Prince are also good-quality canned sardines and are more available and cheaper. Because canned sardines are already cleaned, you'll need less—about 12 ounces for this dish.

Salt

2 to 3 cups cauliflower florets

1/2 teaspoon saffron threads

1 tablespoon tomato paste

2 tablespoons currants or raisins*

1 pound bucatini, perciatelli, or the pasta of your choice

2 fennel bulbs (chose ones with the leafiest fronds)

1/3 cup olive oil (if using fresh sardines)

1 pound fresh sardines, cleaned and each cut into 2 fillets; or 12 ounces of drained canned sardines

1 small onion, chopped fine (1/2 cup or less)

1 clove garlic, chopped fine

5 anchovy fillets, chopped

1/4 cup pine nuts, lightly toasted*

Pepper

Pinch (or more) of red pepper flakes (optional)

1/2 cup unflavored bread crumbs, lightly toasted

1. Bring 4 quarts of water to a boil. Add 1 teaspoon salt, stir, and add the cauliflower. Cook just until tender, 3 or 4 minutes. Remove with a skimmer or strainer to a bowl. Set aside.

2. Remove one cup of water from the pot, and put it in a small bowl with the saffron and tomato paste. Blend thoroughly. Add the currants or raisins, and set aside.

3. Return the pot of water (used to cook the cauliflower) to a boil. Add another teaspoon of salt and the pasta. Cook just until al dente.

4. While the pasta cooks, remove the leafy fronds from the tops of the fennel bulbs and chop. If you don't have 2 cups worth, finely chop the thinner green tops and some of the white bulbs to give you what you need. (Use the remaining bulbs for another purpose, such as a crudité platter.)

5. If using fresh sardines, put a large sauté pan or Dutch oven over medium heat. Add the olive oil. When hot, add the sardine fillets in batches, so as not to crowd the pan. Sauté quickly on both sides, just until they lose color. They shouldn't cook all the way through. Remove to a plate. (Disregard this step if you are using canned sardines.)

6. Add the onions to the pan used for the fresh sardines, and gently sauté. (If you are using canned sardines, add the oil you would have used in step 5 before adding the onions.) When the onions become translucent, add the garlic and anchovies, mashing the anchovies with the back of a spoon. Add the saffron, tomato paste, and currant (or raisin) mixture. Add the fennel, pine nuts, and cauliflower. Blend

well but gently, and cook until the sauce just begins to thicken. Then add the cooked (or canned) sardines. (If the canned sardines are fairly large, you can cut them in half.)

7. When the pasta is done, scoop out and set aside a cup of the cooking water. Then drain the pasta thoroughly. Add the pasta to the sauce. Toss well and taste for seasoning. Add salt and pepper to taste, and red pepper flakes, if desired. Add a little of the reserved cooking water if the mixture seems too dry. Add the bread crumbs and toss again. Serves 4 (or more as part of a St. Joseph's table or buffet).

No need to hurry when serving this dish. In fact, it improves as it sits, with flavors blending together nicely. I think it's best served warm, but it's also quite good at room temperature, which is the way you'll see it on a St. Joseph's table.

* Recipe Note: Some versions of pasta con sarde use sultana raisins and toasted almonds.

HAVE A COOKIE

When I was growing up, Christmastime was cookie time. And no one made cookies like my aunt Sandy.

Aunt Sandy was the aunt-at-large to all of us nieces and nephews. Rather than get married, she took care of her mother until Grandma died. Then she moved upstairs from my mother.

Almost every Italian family I ever knew had a maiden aunt. Sometimes instead of a maiden aunt, the family might have a woman who married young, was widowed, never remarried, and wore black for the rest of her life. The only thing black about Aunt Sandy was her hair, which we all swore she dyed to cover the gray.

Aunt Sandy's real name was Santina. But her name, like so many other very Italian names, was changed to be something more American. Aunt Sandy also had two cousins named Santina. Since we often saw the other Santinas at large family gatherings—most of our family gatherings were large—they were called Sa or Sah, though I doubt anyone ever spelled it.

It was a bit confusing to have two other Santinas called Sa (or Sah). But one wasn't married (and had a serious, very Italian-looking mole on her cheek). The other was married to Vinnie, who was as short as his wife. That helped.

Before becoming disabled, Aunt Sandy made about twenty kinds of cookies, every one a knockout. There were coral islands, light and tender with strawberry jam centers; butterballs, round, rich nuggets coated with powdered sugar; *giuggiuleni*, miniature footballs covered with toasted sesame seeds; mocha nut crescents, flavored with cocoa and coffee; and triangles (also known as English toffee bars), thin, crisp wafers with walnuts and a hint of cinnamon.

During the holidays, these cookies were augmented by my mother's *cucciddati*, traditional Italian Christmas cookies stuffed with ground dates and figs. According to food historian Waverly Root, in Palermo they also contain almond cream, candied squash, and bits of chocolate. The Guginos came from a town southeast of Palermo called Valledolmo. Mom's family came from Racalmuto, a small town near Agrigento in southeastern Sicily.

After the cucciddati were baked, they were iced and sprinkled with nonpareils. Mom always reserved a batch of unfrosted cookies for my father. Dad thought the addition of frosting and sugary sprinkles on cookies was unnecessary because the cookies were already too rich—the crust alone had lard, shortening, *and* eggs.

Mom and Aunt Sandy would make up little trays of their cookies on paper plates lined with doilies. Butterballs were ensconced in small, frilly, colored paper cups so their powdered-sugar coatings wouldn't get on the other cookies. Then the plates were covered with clear plastic wrap and tied with red and green ribbons.

These packages were destined for relatives, whom Mom would drag us to visit. Often, they were distant cousins we hadn't seen since the last wake and had no real interest in seeing again.

"Who are we going to see tonight, Mom?"

"Cousin Phil."

"Who's Cousin Phil?"

"You know Cousin Phil. He's Grandma's second cousin, on her mother's side."

"That doesn't tell me anything. Have I met him before?"

"Sure you have, at Cousin Carmela's wedding."

"Who's Cousin Carmela?"

When people came to our house for a holiday visit, they always found a plate or two of cookies on the dining room table. Mom would greet the guests with "How about some schnapps?" I have no idea why a Sicilian woman asked other Sicilians if they wanted schnapps, which was originally a clear Austrian fruit brandy. Our "schnapps" was usually a bottle of anisette, a clear licorice-tasting liqueur that we drank only during the holidays. That bottle of anisette lasted longer than most marriages.

In addition to Dad's fondness for unfrosted cucciddati, we each had our favorite cookie. I liked triangles (after an early preference for butterballs). My brother Frank was partial to giuggiuleni. Russ loved butterballs.

Aunt Sandy also made cookies for weddings, christenings, and first Communions. Considering the size of the extended family, that's a lot of cookies. The demand was so great that Aunt Sandy had to set up a pecking order. She decreed that all thirteen nieces and nephews automatically got them for all occasions. Second cousins and their children got them only for weddings. Third cousins got them only when they died.

A few years before she became bedridden, we realized that Aunt Sandy wouldn't be with us forever. So, some of my cousins, my sister Maria, and I set out to learn the secrets from the cookie queen.

Aunt Sandy kept her cookie recipes in an envelope in the pantry near the cornflakes, though written recipes were superfluous. Aunt Sandy had long since committed the recipes to memory.

Even the concept of a recipe was loosely defined when it came to Aunt Sandy's cookies. Take shortening, for example. Aunt Sandy worked with shortening, an essential ingredient in much of her baking, so often that she eschewed normal measuring devices in favor of a wooden spoon.

"I take my spoon and scoop out some shortening," she said. "Then I look at it and say, 'This looks like a cup.'"

Her brownie recipe reflected a similar casualness. I asked her how much chopped walnuts (another favorite ingredient) she used in her recipe.

"I put in whatever I have. Sometimes I have more, and I put in more. Sometimes I have less, so I use less," she said nonchalantly.

Then there was the whole issue of margarine versus butter. Aunt Sandy used margarine, even in the butterballs. "Butter is too expensive," she said. "Besides, my cookies are rich enough without it." This was long before trans fats in margarine were shown to be a greater risk for coronary heart disease than butter. Of course, there are now many margarines made without trans fats. Some even claim to be so much like butter that one couldn't tell the difference. I've tried a few. Not bad. But I'd rather use butter.

I don't bake as often as Mom and Aunt Sandy did. So, some of what follows might sound obvious to regular bakers. Don't crowd the cookies, or they may run into each other. The recipes below will make anywhere from two to four dozen cookies, which means you either need more than one cookie sheet or you'll have to wait until the first batch cools before making the second batch. However, you don't need to bake all the cookies at once. The dough will keep in the fridge for a week or so, much longer in the freezer. (I froze the dough and filling for the cucciddati for more than six months with no deleterious effects.)

CORAL ISLANDS

Some folks will recognize these cookies by another name, thumbprints, named for the indentation made by the thumb, which is filled with jam. (Little Aunt Jo—more on Little and Big Aunt Jo later—called them jamborees.) Since everyone's thumb is different, I used the back of a half-teaspoon measure to make the indent instead.

2/3 cup butter

1/3 cup brown sugar

1 egg, separated

1 teaspoon almond extract

1 1/3 cups all-purpose flour, approximately, sifted

1/2 cup finely chopped walnuts

Strawberry or raspberry preserves, about 1 cup

1. Heat the oven to 350 degrees.

2. In a mixing bowl, cream the butter and sugar with an electric mixer. Add the egg yolk and almond extract and beat well. Gradually add the flour and blend well. After you've used almost all of the flour, test to see if the dough is pliable but not too sticky. Add more flour, if needed.

3. Shape the dough into 1-inch balls. Lightly beat the egg white so that it is still slightly runny. Put the walnuts in a bowl nearby. Dip half of each ball into the egg white. Then dip that part into the nuts. Place on a cookie sheet, nut side up, and make a depression with the back of a half-teaspoon measure. It should be just deep enough to hold a little less than 1/2 teaspoon of preserves. Fill the depression with preserves. Bake until lightly browned, 15 to 20 minutes. Makes about 25 cookies.

TRIANGLES (ENGLISH TOFFEE BARS)

When I first tested this recipe, I thought that the dimensions of the pan Aunt Sandy used in this recipe—15 1/2 x 10 1/2 x 1 inch—seemed a bit odd. Unfortunately, Aunt Sandy was no longer available to explain why. So I googled those dimensions and found out those are the dimensions of a jelly roll pan. (Aunt Sandy's recipe just said "pan.") I also discovered that not all jelly roll pans have the same dimensions. The first five I found varied in width from 9 1/2 inches to 13 inches; the lengths from 14 to 18 inches. Then I consulted the greatest cookie and cake maker of all time, the late Maida Heater. Or, rather, one of her books, which has a similar recipe for cinnamon almond cookies. Lo and behold, she called for the same size pan as Aunt Sandy!

That said, you don't need to use a pan with any of those exact dimensions. All you need is one that has a total of 160 square inches, which is just about what Aunt Sandy's—and Maida Heater's—was. (In case you forgot your elementary school math, multiply the width by the length to get the square inches.) Aunt Sandy also cut her cookies into pieces, 2 1/4 inches by 2 inches. I have no idea why, but her recipe states this yields approximately 70 cookies when those pieces are cut in half on the diagonal to make triangles. It's a lot easier if those pieces are 2-inches square before cutting, which would technically give you 80 cookies, if you are absolutely accurate. But given the variables and the inevitable mishaps we all make, figure 70–80.

Finally, a few tips from the meticulous Maida Heater. While I figured out that wax paper would help in spreading the dough in the pan—Aunt Sandy may have had her own method—Heater suggests using a straight-sided glass like a rolling pin to smooth out the dough. (I used an old Illy coffee canister.) She also suggests the same method for pressing the walnuts into the dough before baking.

1 cup softened butter, plus more for greasing the pan or butter-flavored spray

1 cup sugar

1 egg, separated

2 cups all-purpose flour, sifted with 1 teaspoon cinnamon

1 cup chopped walnuts

1. Heat the oven to 275 degrees.

2. In a large mixing bowl, cream the butter using a handheld mixer or standing mixer. Gradually add the sugar, and beat until light and fluffy. Beat in the egg yolk. Gradually add the seasoned flour to the butter mixture. Combine thoroughly.

3. Using softened butter or butter-flavored spray, lightly grease a baking pan that measures 160 square inches. Put the dough onto the pan and cover with wax paper. Press the dough into the pan with your hands or with a straight-sided large glass or coffee can. Make sure the dough is evenly distributed.

4. Lightly beat the egg white and brush it on top of the dough. Spread the walnuts evenly over the dough. Then gently press the nuts into the dough using the glass or coffee can.

5. Bake for 1 hour.* While still hot from the oven, cut the baked dough in the pan into 2-inch squares. You should have about 35 squares. Cut each square diagonally so that you have 70 triangles. Gently lift from the pan with a spatula, and let cool. Makes 70 to 80 cookies.

*Since my wife thought an hour seemed a long baking time for this recipe, I thought I'd assure you that the timing is correct. Remember, the oven temperature is only 275 degrees.

Giuggiuleni (photo credit, Maryann Bolles)

GIUGGIULENI

Giuggiuleni are sesame cookies shaped like mini footballs, at least the way Aunt Sandy made them. Many recipes for giuggiuleni, however, are for nougat candies, also with sesame seeds, though in a variety of shapes. Some recipes contain almonds and a few colored candied sprinkles, like the kind Mom used on cuccidati. The name giuggiuleni, or giurgiuleni—there are other spellings as well—derives from the Arab *juljulàn* or *giolgiolan,* meaning sesame, not surprising since so many dishes in Sicily have Arab influences.

Giuggiuleni (the singular is giuggiulena) are not as sweet as Aunt Sandy's other cookies and are a little dry, though intentionally so, much like biscotti. As with biscotti, they're great for dunking in coffee or hot chocolate. And I find them a nice contrast to the sweeter cookies.

My cousin Maryann Bolles (who made the mistake of marrying a MeriCAHN when she was just a teenager; it didn't last) told me that when she made them, "I was transported to your mom's kitchen and the big cookie jar always full of them!"

When Mom made these cookies after Aunt Sandy died, she dipped the dough balls in a combination of beaten eggs and milk before rolling them in sesame seeds. I've found that step unnecessary. The seeds adhere to the dough just fine, and eliminating the egg wash makes the process a lot less messy. I found no difference in taste.

As with loaves of bread, you will often see some cracking on top of the giuggiuleni when they are done. This is from the dough spreading as it cooks. Though I have no problem with the cracks, if you want more perfect-looking cookies, try shaping the dough when it's cold. Another tip is to line your cookie sheets with silicone mats. I've tried both. And while they help, I still got some cracks.

1 cup vegetable shortening

3/4 cup sugar

2 eggs

2 tablespoons baking powder

1 teaspoon vanilla

2 tablespoons milk

3 1/2 to 4 cups all-purpose flour, sifted

2 cups sesame seeds

1. Preheat the oven to 375 degrees.

2. In a mixing bowl, cream the shortening with an electric mixer. Add the sugar, and beat until well combined. Add the eggs, the baking powder, vanilla, and milk, making sure each is fully incorporated before adding the next one. Gradually add the flour until you have used 3 1/2 cups. When the flour has been completely mixed in, check the consistency of the dough. It should be smooth and somewhat pliable but not too sticky. If too sticky or soft, add the remaining 1/2 cup of flour, a tablespoon at a time.

3. Shape the dough into balls 1-inch in diameter. Put the sesame seeds in a small bowl. Roll the balls in the sesame seeds. Shape with your hand into 1 3/4- to 2-inch oblong shapes, like little footballs. Bake for 20 minutes, and check to see if the cookies are nicely browned on the bottom. If not, bake an additional 5 minutes. The tops of the cookies should be golden brown. Makes 50 to 60 cookies.

Mom's Fig cookies (cucidatti) oven 350°

1 lb shortening (not oleo) 2 cups
1 lb sugar 2 cups
9 eggs
5 tbsp baking powder
1 orange juice & rind
Enough flour to make med. dough.

Filling
1 lb. figs
1 pkg. pitted dates } ground together
1 orange juice & rind
1 cup toasted walnut (chopped not ground)
1 tbsp cinnamon
½ cup sugar
½ cup water

Heat until sugar has dissolved (cool).

(over)   350° oven

Mom's handwritten recipe for cucciddati

MOM'S CUCCIDDATI

While Aunt Sandy was the acknowledged cookie master, Mom was the maven of cucciddati. I can still recall her grinding the dates and figs in a meat grinder attached to the kitchen table. If you don't have a meat grinder or meat grinder attachment for your standing mixer, you'll probably use a food processor. In that case, grind them in two or more batches to make sure they are thoroughly ground. Adding the orange juice and rind while grinding can also make the process go a bit smoother. Regardless of which method you use, halve the dates before grinding because, invariably, there will be a pit, despite what the label says.

Dough

1/2 cup lard

1/2 cup vegetable shortening

1 cup sugar

5 eggs

3 tablespoons baking powder

Juice and grated rind from
   one small orange

4 1/2 to 5 cups flour

Filling

1 pound pitted dates, halved

1 pound dried Calimyrna figs,
   stems removed*

1/2 cup chopped walnuts

Juice and rind of one small
   orange

1/4 cup sugar

1/4 cup water

Frosting

3 tablespoons softened butter

3 cups powdered sugar

6 tablespoons or more whole
   milk

Nonpareils (multicolored
   sprinkles)

1. For the dough, cream the lard and shortening in a mixing bowl with an electric mixer. (The paddle attachment of a standing mixer works best here.) Add the sugar and mix well. Add the eggs, baking powder, orange juice, and rind, and mix well. Add 4 1/2 cups of the flour gradually, with the mixer on low speed, until you achieve a pliable dough. If too sticky, add more flour, a tablespoon at a time. Cover in plastic wrap and refrigerate while you prepare the filling.

2. For the filling, grind the dates and figs together. Put the dates and figs in a heavy-bottom saucepan with remaining filling ingredients. Stir over low heat so that the sugar completely dissolves and the mixture is smooth and spreadable, about 15 minutes. Cool.

3. Heat the oven to 350 degrees. To assemble, roll out dough to a thickness of about 1/8 to 3/16 inch. (If it's too soft, put the dough in the freezer for 5 minutes or so to stiffen.) Cut the dough into strips about 8 to 10 inches long and 2 1/2 inches wide. Put the filling down the center of each dough strip, lengthwise. The amount of the filling should be somewhat less than a third of the width of the dough, just enough so that both sides of the dough will easily meet when wrapped over the filling. Then fold each side of the dough over the filling. Press down on the seam to seal. Cut the cookies into 2-inch lengths on a slight diagonal. Put cookies on a baking sheet, seam side down. Bake for 12 to 15 minutes until slightly browned. Cool.

4. While the cookies are baking, make the frosting by beating the butter with 1 cup of the powdered sugar. (Don't beat too vigorously or some of the powdered sugar will fly out of the bowl.) Add the remaining sugar, 1 cup at a time, until well blended. Gradually add the milk, 1 tablespoon at a time, until you get a smooth, slightly runny consistency. When cookies are cool, frost with a knife, and sprinkle with nonpareils. Makes about 10 dozen cookies. Freeze with or without frosting.

* Dried Calimyrna figs usually come from Turkey or California. Calimyrna figs from Turkey (sometimes just labeled "Turkish figs") are lighter in color. They're also drier and more leathery than California figs. Use the latter if you have a choice.

How to store these cookies

Whether you're storing them in or out of the freezer, make sure the cookies are first cooled to room temperature. When storing at room temperature, put the cookies in a container with a tight-fitting lid. (Like a cookie tin!) They should keep a few weeks if kept somewhat cooler than room temperature (like the room under the stairs at Grandma and Aunt Sandy's house; see "More on Aunt Sandy's Cookies" pg 129)

Cookies can be frozen for up to six months if separated in layers with foil or plastic wrap in a tightly sealed container. To thaw cookies, put them on a serving plate loosely covered for about 20 minutes.

ITALIAN MEDICINE

Jews refer to chicken soup as Jewish penicillin. My mother's chicken soup was penicillin on steroids. It's so good we frequently had it in place of spaghetti on Sunday. That may not sound like such a big deal to you, but a Sunday *sensa sugo* could prompt withdrawal symptoms. Fortunately, Mom's chicken soup, which was really a soup dinner—you didn't think just soup was enough, did you?—was immensely satisfying. And there was always a pot of sauce in the downstairs fridge in case we started crawling up the walls.

The making and eating of chicken soup is filled with tradition and warm memories. Mom always made chicken soup on a Sunday. The wafting aromas would fill the house on Sunday morning as we got ready for church. Sunday dinner was usually served around one or two o'clock in the afternoon, depending on what time the football games started on television.

As the chicken simmered, my brothers and I would vie for the hearts, gizzards, and unborn eggs (tiny egg yolks). Can you imagine kids today fighting with their siblings over these outré parts?

Once the chicken was tender, it was removed to a roasting pan and baked. Tiny macaroni and peas were added to the soup to make a hearty first course. Mom also made an onion and potato dish that was simple and satisfying. Throw in a salad (God forbid we should go through a meal without some roughage), and you've got a great Sunday dinner.

After I went away to college, we stopped having chicken soup. I asked my mother why. She said, "They don't make those kinds of chickens anymore."

What were "those kinds of chickens"? You've heard the expression "tough old bird"? Well, that's what you need for soup chicken. A frying chicken is no good because after an hour or so, it will fall apart. A soup chicken has more character. It will hang in there until a good stock is made.

Before I was ten, we lived in an old Italian neighborhood, which had a poultry shop right next to my elementary school. A poultry shop in those days carried live chickens in wooden crates. You want chicken for dinner? Then one of those birds has to meet his maker, right there in the shop. Sometimes my mother and grandmother would buy live chickens and take them home. But I never thought about how those live chickens got to be dead, cooked chickens on our dinner table until I was several years older.

The poultry store became an auto body shop. And we moved to a new neighborhood with very few Italians and no live chickens. One Saturday morning, Mom came home from the Fillmore Farmers' Market with an irresistible bargain—ten live chickens! (For Mom, a bargain wasn't a bargain unless you bought a lot. So two, or three, or even five chickens wouldn't do.) In addition to the volume she purchased, I'm guessing the farmer who sold the chickens to Mom gave her a good deal because not many people knew what to do with these old birds.

Unfortunately for me and my brothers, we weren't aware of what Mom was bringing home from the farmers' market. Otherwise, we'd have been playing football somewhere in another ZIP code. But we were home when Mom arrived and announced, "Boys, I've got some work for you."

In a bizarre performance that only could have been written and choreographed by Mel Brooks and Boris Karloff, we proceeded to send ten chickens to their final resting places. It might have been easier if the axe my brother Frank used (made by my father, a welder) had been sharper, but at least it was heavy. My job was only slightly less gruesome—holding the headless chickens upside down by the legs in a bucket until they stopped moving. Since that day, the term "running around like a chicken with its head cut off" has had a whole new meaning for me. Younger brother, Russ, had a less grisly, though more tedious, task. He was the plucker.

I wish I could say those birds were worth the effort, but they weren't. As a final irony—and perhaps a curse on their executioners—they refused to soften up under normal cooking procedures. I'm sure there's a moral there somewhere.

Today, the antiseptic ways in which we buy food aren't as much fun. My wife, Mary, swears that chicken—and food, in general—doesn't taste like it used to. That may be so. It certainly is more difficult to get a soup chicken. However, if you do find some live ones, I have a slightly used axe I can lend you.

CHICKEN SOUP

For most people, the soup chickens of my youth aren't available. Instead, look for a stewing chicken, which is usually a hen that has passed its prime egg-laying days and is anywhere from ten months to one and a half years old versus seven to ten weeks for a typical fryer. Look for them in good butcher or poultry shops, ethnic markets, and farmers' markets.

To coordinate the soup, chicken, and potatoes, do the following: about 20 minutes before the stock is done, prepare the potatoes up to when they are put into the oven. Put the potatoes and chicken in the oven at the same time. While the soup is finishing, prepare a salad.

For the Stock

1 whole stewing chicken, about 7 pounds, with giblets

3 medium onions, peeled and halved

3 ribs of celery with leaves, cut into 2-inch pieces

3 large carrots, peeled and cut into 2-inch pieces (longer at the narrower end of the carrot)

2 large fresh tomatoes, halved, or 1 (28-ounce) can of tomatoes, drained

8–10 parsley stems

2 bay leaves

10 whole peppercorns

1 teaspoon paprika

1. Remove the giblets from the chicken. Set the liver aside for another use. (If you buy enough whole chickens, the accumulated frozen livers can be made into a pâté.)

2. Put the chicken and vegetables in a large pot. Wrap the parsley stems, bay leaves, and peppercorns in cheesecloth and add to the pot. Fill with 8 quarts of water.

3. Heat until just before it reaches a full boil; skim the foam that forms on the surface with a ladle. Skim it a few more times as the stock simmers for about 2 hours or until chicken is barely tender. (Be careful not to overcook the chicken, or it will fall apart when you remove it. If you're not sure about doneness, use an instant-read thermometer. The breast should be 155 to 160 degrees.)

4. About 20 minutes before the stock is done, scoop out 1/2 cup of the stock and set aside for the potatoes. Prepare the potatoes up to when they are put into the oven. (See below.)

5. Heat the oven to 350 degrees.

6. Remove the chicken to a roasting pan, reserving the stock. Sprinkle the chicken with paprika and bake, covered, for 30 minutes before serving.

For the Soup

6 ounces tubettini, pastina, ditalini, or similar small macaroni

8 ounces frozen peas, defrosted

Salt and pepper to taste

Grated Romano or Parmigiano cheese or a combination of both

1. While the chicken is baking, strain the stock through cheesecloth. Reserve the carrots for the soup and 1/2 cup stock for the potatoes. (See below.) Save the heart, gizzard, and neck for snacking. Reduce the stock to about 3 1/2 quarts. (While the stock is reducing, start the potatoes.)

2. When the stock has been reduced, add the macaroni, and cook for 5 minutes. Add peas and cook for 5 minutes. Meanwhile, cut the carrots into 1/2-inch cubes. Add them to the soup.

3. Season to taste with salt and pepper.

4. Serve hot with plenty of grated cheese as a first course, followed by the chicken, roasted potatoes, and a tossed salad. The soup serves about 10 and reheats well.

ROASTED POTATOES WITH ONIONS

3 tablespoons butter (or more, if needed)

2 tablespoons olive oil (or more, if needed)

6 large potatoes (3 to 3 1/2 pounds), peeled and cut into 1 1/2- to 2-inch chunks

3 large onions (about 1 1/2 pounds), peeled and thinly sliced

Cooking oil spray or additional olive oil

1/2 cup chicken stock from the above recipe

Salt and pepper to taste

1. Put a large frying pan over medium heat. Add the butter and oil. When the butter stops sizzling, add the potatoes in one layer without crowding the pan. (This may have to be done in batches if your pan isn't big enough.) Raise the heat to medium-high.

2. Fry the potatoes until well browned (about 10 minutes), turning frequently to prevent burning. Season with salt and pepper.

3. Meanwhile, grease an ovenproof dish with cooking oil spray (or olive oil), and turn the oven to 350 degrees.

4. When the potatoes are browned, add them to the baking dish with a slotted spoon, leaving any oil or butter in the pan.

5. Lower the frying pan heat to medium. Add a tablespoon of oil or butter, if needed. Add the onions, and cook until lightly brown, stirring periodically to prevent burning, about 10 minutes. Season with salt and pepper. Spoon the onions over the potatoes with a slotted spoon.

6. Add the chicken stock to the frying pan. Season the liquid with salt and pepper. Raise the heat, and boil a few minutes. Pour over the potatoes and onions and stir everything together.

7. Bake covered for 30 minutes or until the potatoes are tender. Serves 6 to 8.

NO THANKS FOR FRIDAYS

Adults look forward to Fridays. "Thank God it's Friday!" they say as they rush out of office buildings, factories, and stores, heading for their favorite watering holes or a weekend at the beach or the mountains. Kids also can't wait for Fridays. It means forgetting about multiplication tables and syntax until Monday morning.

I was never a big fan of Fridays. You see, when I was growing up, Fridays meant only one thing—no meat.

When you say *no meat* in my family, you're saying no to Genoa salami, braciola, spareribs, baked ham, steak, meatballs, sausage, lamb chops, pepperoni, capicola, mortadella, lamb stew, pork chops, ham hocks, roast chicken, and tripe. In short, you're saying no to everything worth living for.

This wasn't a minor inconvenience. This was one-seventh of your week. This was pain. How painful? It was the pain of being sent to your room, when your room had only a bed, to "wait until your father comes home" for punishment you dared not contemplate. It was the pain of finally realizing you just traded your Mickey Mantle baseball card for Hoyt Wilhelm and Minnie Miñoso.

The Catholic Church lifted its ban on Friday meat-eating in 1966. It was just my luck that I was leaving the church (and home to go to college in Philadelphia) about that time. I had tolerated a lot from the church. I went to catechism every Monday to be given a list of don'ts. I avoided movies that were condemned by the Legion of Decency. I tried not to think impure thoughts. But this meat ban was the limit.

The reasons for the meat ban were never entirely made clear to us by the church, though the priests and nuns always seemed to have an answer, however oblique, for our queries about Fridays and other questionable church practices and traditions.

Example: Otto Sticka was a wise guy in my catechism class. (And a pole vaulter in high school. There must be some kind of connection.) On this particular Monday, the priest was talking about suicide being a mortal sin, meaning a nonstop ticket to hell. In an earlier class, the priest said that if one died wearing a scapular, one would escape the fiery abyss. A scapular is two small, rectangular pieces of cloth or laminated paper with religious pictures on them, connected by a ribbon or string, which is worn like a kind of necklace. Otto's hand shot up. "What if a guy jumped off a bridge to commit suicide but he was wearing a scapular," asked Otto. "Would he still go to heaven?" The priest thought for a few moments and said, "In the fall from the bridge, the scapular would have come off, and the person would go to hell."

Historians tell us that meatless Fridays started centuries ago as a sacrifice to remind Catholics of the suffering of Jesus on Good Friday. (Not, as many thought, to give a boost to a sagging fishing industry in Italy.) Eating fish wasn't encouraged, but it was a logical alternative to meat. So fish became a popular meat substitute on Fridays.

However, we weren't fish eaters, which was odd because both sides of my family are Sicilian. And in Sicily, fishing is a big industry. As Waverly Root noted in his book *The Food of Italy*, "Sicilians do not go in much for meat, partly because they do not raise much." And, of course, Sicily is surrounded by the Mediterranean. But when Sicilian immigrants came to the United States, they found a bounty of meat and poultry, much cheaper than what it cost in their native country.

The only exception to our general aversion to fish was the Friday "fish fry," the American equivalent of fish and chips, which was available at almost every family restaurant, diner, and tavern in the Buffalo area. If money wasn't so tight in my family, we would have gone out for a fish fry more often. As it was, a visit to a restaurant for a fish fry happened about once every leap year. Similarly, fish prepared at home was limited to things like whiting and haddock. The only time you ate shrimp was when you had a shrimp cocktail before your filet mignon at your senior prom dinner or when you got married.

There was one exception to the fish phobia. But it wasn't fish, or seafood of any kind, though we thought it was. And in the dogma of the Catholic Church, if you *thought* you weren't committing a sin, you weren't *really* committing a sin. Thus, for example, complete idiots could eat meat every Friday.

The "seafood" we loved to eat was snails. I'm not sure why Mom thought snails were seafood. They were displayed live in straw-lined barrels in the Italian grocery store where we shopped. Somehow, that obvious fact never connected. Either that or Mom knew snails weren't seafood all along but was desperate to satisfy her carnivorous family on Fridays.

Our ignorance, therefore, enabled us to eat meat in the form of snails on Fridays. The snails were so good it should have been a tip-off that there was a reason. They were meat! We were too busy with our toothpicks and straightened-out paper clips, prying the reluctant snails out of their shells. Or sopping up the great sauce with bread. These weren't escargot, the garlicky French appetizer served in a ramekin. Those snails were larger and more easily removed from their shells. The snails used in the Sicilian main dish called *babbalucci* were smaller and served in a tomato sauce.

Babbalucci (also spelled *babbaluci*), a word we never used in my family, is Sicilian slang for snails. The smaller snails in babbalucci sometimes made it difficult to extract the meat from the shell. But Mom had a solution. She put the live snails in a pot of cool water over a low flame and slowly increased the heat. The snails got used to the water gradually and began to come out of their shells. By the time the water was hot, the snails had swelled and couldn't get back into their shells. At least that's the way Mom explained it.

Today, finding live snails, like the ones Mom used in babbalucci, is as difficult as finding bacon in a mosque. Almost all snails are cooked and sold in cans, though some also come with shells with which you can create *escargots de bourgogne*, the French dish with garlic, butter, and parsley. Peconic Escargot (peconicescargot.com) raises snails on Long Island. They are sold fresh, meaning they aren't alive but not cooked—like fish! However, they are expensive, $40 for 48 snails, plus $25 for shipping. That sound you hear is Mom turning over in her grave.

But we couldn't have snails every Friday. Thus, going (you'll pardon the expression) "cold turkey" by abstaining from meat created a certain amount of tension. The burden fell on Mom's shoulders. She was treated like the messenger who brought the bad news. In other words, it was her fault.

Oddly, Mom did some of her best and most creative cooking on Fridays, though it went unrecognized and unappreciated. She'd work all day on an endless variety of meatless dishes, hoping one would mollify our discomfort. No chance. Her family of hulking carnivores would come home grunting and groaning, hoping against hope for that fix of flesh we knew we couldn't get. We'd ask Mom what was for dinner, knowing full well that it wouldn't include meat, and we'd be disappointed.

I remember once getting the bright idea that if Mom cooked everything *else* she would normally cook for a non-Friday meal, except meat, it would work out just fine. It didn't. The reason is simple. When you ask someone what's for dinner, does that person reply, "Peas and carrots" or even "Potatoes au gratin"? No. It's "We're having fried chicken" or "I made a pot roast." That is, unless you were a vegetarian or, worse, a vegan, both of which we didn't even want to think about. So when we had to go meatless on Friday, the answer to the question "What are we having for dinner?" went something like this:

"We're having artichokes stuffed with onions, fried cauliflower, and pasta fagioli."

"What else?"

"Ah, spaghetti with marinara sauce and hard-boiled eggs and fried cardoons."

"And?"

"Well, ah, asparagus omelet, homemade pizza, and salad."

"Oh. No meat, huh?"

In addition to haddock and whiting we occasionally had smelts on Fridays. Only the smelts stand out as something I remember liking. Since becoming a food writer, I've noticed smelts served as an appetizer, often with a kind of aioli (garlicky mayonnaise) in lieu of tartar sauce. Or as part of the Italian dish *fritto misto*—a mix of fried seafood (usually including squid and shrimp) and sometimes vegetables, like zucchini. (If my family had come from Venice, that would have solved the Friday problem because the Venetians are masters at fritto misto and fried seafood in general.)

On special occasions, like a St. Joseph's table, we might also have squid, either stuffed and baked or fried. Smelts were easy to prepare, but squid took a lot of work. And it was messy. Fortunately, you can easily buy squid cleaned and ready to cook these days, though in supermarkets it's usually frozen.

FRIED SMELTS

Smelts are typically sold ready to cook, except for, perhaps, the fins and tails, which can be snipped off. You may or may not want to remove the backbone. It's so small, many people eat it with the rest of the fish, as we did. The backbone also helps to keep the fish together during cooking.

1 pound smelts

Salt and pepper to taste

Canola or grapeseed oil for frying

1/2 cup flour

Lemon wedges

1. Clip the fins and tails from the smelts.

2. Wash the smelts under cool running water. Leave them wet. Season with salt and pepper to taste.

3. Put a medium to large skillet over medium-high heat. Add the oil to a depth of 1 inch. Heat until the oil is hot but not smoking.

4. Meanwhile, put the flour in a shallow bowl or soup plate, and season with salt and pepper. Dredge the smelts in the flour. Shake off any excess flour, and put them in the skillet. (Take care to remove as much extra flour as you can, or it can collect at the bottom of the pan and make frying later batches more difficult.) Do not crowd the pan.

5. Cook smelts until lightly browned on each side, about 2 minutes total. Don't overcook. Drain on paper towels. Serve immediately with lemon wedges. Serves 4 as an appetizer or 2 as an entrée.

BAKED CALAMARI

Unless you are buying squid from a fish monger (and maybe even if you are), it is likely to be frozen, though cleaned.

8 medium or 12 small squid, cleaned

2 tablespoons olive oil

3 tablespoons chopped parsley

1 teaspoon finely chopped garlic

3 tablespoons freshly grated Parmigiano

3/4 cup plain breadcrumbs

1 egg, lightly beaten

Salt and pepper to taste

1 recipe for pizza sauce (see page 152)

1. Cut off the tentacles from the squid and chop them coarsely. Combine them with all other ingredients except the sauce. If the mixture is too crumbly, add a little water.

2. Heat the oven to 325 degrees.

3. Fill the squid bodies with the mixture but not too tightly, or the squid will burst while cooking. Secure the end with toothpicks.

4. Put a thin layer of sauce in the bottom of a shallow baking dish, large enough to hold the stuffed squid in one layer. Put the squid in and cover with remaining sauce. Cover and bake for 40 minutes. Serves 4.

FRIED CALAMARI

These fried calamari make a great first course served with tartar sauce or just lemon. (Some restaurants serve this dish with a marinara sauce, which I think is too heavy for the delicate calamari.)

1 1/2 pounds cleaned squid

Salt and pepper to taste

1 cup flour

Vegetable oil for frying

Lemon wedges (optional)

1. Cut the sacs of the squid into rings, about 1/2 inch wide. Cut tentacles in two, crosswise. Season with salt and pepper.

2. Put the flour in a shallow bowl or soup plate, and season well with salt and pepper.

3. Put a skillet over medium-high heat. Add the oil to a depth of 1 inch. Heat until the oil is hot but not smoking.

4. Meanwhile, dredge the squid in the flour, and shake off any excess. Add pieces to the pan and fry until golden brown on both sides. Do not crowd the pan.

5. Drain squid on paper towels, and serve immediately with lemon wedges, if desired. Serves 4 as an appetizer.

STUFFED SARDINES

Fresh sardines can be difficult to get in most parts of the country. If you're persistent and especially if you live on the East Coast, you'll probably be able to find them eventually. Whether or not you like canned sardines, you should try fresh sardines at least once. Fresh sardines have a subtle and sweet flavor that makes them taste like different fish from the ones that are canned. (See also "Lent" for pasta con sarde—spaghetti with sardine sauce.)

12 whole, fresh sardines

Salt and pepper to taste

Stuffing from Baked
    Calamari recipe

3/4 cup flour

Vegetable oil for frying

Lemon wedges

1. Make a slit down the belly of each fish. Remove and discard the innards. Lay the fish open and remove the backbone. Clip off any small fins or hairs with scissors. Rinse the fish inside and out under cool, running water. Pat the insides dry. Season the inside cavity of each fish with salt and pepper to taste.

2. Stuff each sardine with about a tablespoon of stuffing. (Don't overstuff.) Secure with toothpicks.

3. Put a skillet large enough to hold all the fish without crowding over medium heat for a few minutes. (You may need to do this in two batches.) Add enough oil to come up to a depth of 1 inch, and heat until the oil is hot but not smoking.

4. Meanwhile, season the flour well with salt and pepper. Roll each fish in the flour. Shake off any excess, and add the fish to the skillet. Fry fish for a few minutes on each side, turning gently. Don't overcook. The fish should be springy (not flakey) to the touch. Drain on a plate lined with paper towels. (If you have to do this dish in batches, put the first batch on an ovenproof platter or pan lined with paper towels in a very low oven to keep warm.) Serve immediately with lemon wedges. Serves 4.

SNAILS (BABBALUCCI)

Though Peconic snails are more expensive, you don't have to go through the arduous process of soaking them and parboiling them before they're ready to be cooked in their sauce, the way Mom did. Use thin metal skewers, the kind you truss a turkey with, to pick out the snails. Serve this dish with plenty of rustic Italian bread and equally rustic Italian red wine.

2 tablespoons olive oil

2 ribs celery, cut into thin (1/4- to 3/8-inch) crescents

1 1/2 cups chopped onions

3 cloves garlic, finely chopped

1 (28-ounce) can Italian plum tomatoes

1 (6-ounce) can tomato paste

2 teaspoons of oregano

2 bay leaves

1/4 cup chopped Italian parsley

1/2 teaspoon red pepper flakes

Salt and pepper to taste

48 raw snails*

3 medium/large potatoes (about 1 1/2 pounds), peeled and cut into 1-inch cubes

1. Put a large heavy-bottom saucepan or Dutch oven over medium heat. Add the oil. When the oil is hot, add the celery, and sauté for 2–3 minutes. Add the onion, and cook just until it softens. Add the garlic, and cook a few minutes more, being careful not to let it burn.

2. Add all the remaining ingredients, except the snails and potatoes. Simmer for 15 minutes.

3. Add the snails, and simmer for 20 minutes. Add the potatoes, and cook until the potatoes are done, about 15 minutes more. Serves 4.

* As of this writing, 48 snails from Peconic Escargot must be ordered by midnight on Monday for delivery on Wednesday. Refrigerated, they keep for 7 to 9 days.

THE PERFECT END TO A MEAL

As an honors graduate of the Mothers Cooking and Eating School, Mom always told us what all mothers told their kids in those days—clean your plate before you can have dessert. This was never a problem. Mom's only worry was making sure we didn't eat the china as well.

Except for my brother Russ. As a finicky eater, Russ was not well understood in our family and was grudgingly tolerated. We reacted to Russ like a Jewish family might react to a child who didn't like chopped liver, pastrami, and knishes.

Russ had a habit of playing with his food. Food was serious business. If it wasn't, why did we clean our plates for the starving people in China? While my older brother, Frank, and I were busy cleaning our plates, Russ was putting mustard in his mashed potatoes and relish in his bacon-and-bean soup.

Russ also had a hard time with vegetables. French fries and mashed potatoes didn't count, maybe because they weren't green, like spinach and broccoli. To be fair, Russ had more of a handicap than most finicky eaters. After all, few families in the 1950s and '60s put artichokes, cardoons, and dandelions on the dinner table. Russ wasn't finicky, however, when it came to desserts.

Desserts were rather hearty fare. Nothing fancy. They were desserts a truck driver might make a detour for or that a diner would serve with pride. Mom made baked apples, rice pudding, chocolate cake, and pies.

Mom's forte was pies, primarily apple, lemon meringue, coconut cream, peach, and pumpkin. Peach pie was especially good but infrequently made because Mom only used fresh peaches. She told me she didn't know how to make it with canned peaches. Ironically, she always made pumpkin pie with canned pumpkin (as it is with most people) and only around Thanksgiving and perhaps into the Christmas holidays, though it was good enough to eat all year long.

The consensus favorite of Mom's pies was coconut cream. Some time ago, my sister, Maria, changed her preference to lemon meringue because "it's lighter." I'm not sure I understand that logic. It's sort of like a running back who prefers getting hit by a 250-pound linebacker rather than by a 300-pound lineman.

When Mom baked pies, she always had some leftover dough, which she rolled out and cut into bite-sized shapes. After being sprinkled with cinnamon and sugar they were baked. They were a real treat, especially when they'd just come out of the oven. When they cooled (if there were any left to cool), they were less scrumptious. This creative use of leftovers was vintage Mom. "It never occurred to me that Mom planned it that way," Maria once told me.

Unlike pizza fritte (see chapter "Traditions"), these little treats didn't have a name. Or if they did, I never knew it. Or I forgot it. So I once asked Frank what we used to call those little leftover pieces of dough from pies. He said, "I thought we called them little leftover pieces of dough from pies." Thanks, Frank.

Mom's heaviest output of pies was during Thanksgiving and Christmas, which meant space was needed for all these desserts after they came out of the oven. Fortunately, we lived in Buffalo, NY, where it got pretty chilly right after Labor Day. This meant Mom could cool her pies in the vestibule, an old-fashioned word for the front hallway or entrance and a word that nobody uses anymore (like davenport, which is what Dad called the sofa). Not only was the vestibule the right temperature, but since no one came through the front door, it was a perfect walk-in cooler.

Mom usually baked coconut cream and lemon meringue pies for holidays. The connection between those pies and Christmas and Thanksgiving remains a mystery to me. As a kid, it seemed perfectly logical. After a traditional Thanksgiving dinner of turkey with all the trimmings, a nice piece of coconut cream pie was, as Dad would say, "just the ticket" to end the meal. If you weren't stuffed before dessert, the weight of even a sliver of pie was enough to send you over the edge. A better sleeping pill has yet to be devised. The entire male contingent was on its way to dreamland as the Green Bay Packers–Detroit Lions game drew to a close on television.

When you get right down to it, the pies Mom made were the pies Dad liked. Mom was from the old school that believed a wife catered to her husband's every whim. Most of Dad's whims involved food. Two of his more memorable quirks were pouring milk over his apple pie and dunking his coconut cream pie in his coffee.

After Dad died in 1966, Mom continued to make coconut cream and other pies for us when we visited. We tended to eat them in a more traditional manner than Dad did, as long as you discount eating coconut cream pie for breakfast.

COCONUT CREAM PIE

It took a few mishaps with pie filling that didn't thicken to realize I hadn't left the eggs out long enough at room temperature before making the filling. Take the eggs out at least 30 minutes before making the pie filling. The other filling problem was that it was almost overflowing the pie crust. I decided to use a slightly deeper 9-inch pie plate and to increase the ingredients in the pie crust a bit.

Pie Crust

1 1/2 cups flour

1/2 teaspoon salt

9 tablespoons well-chilled shortening

4–6 tablespoons ice water

Filling

1/2 cup sugar

1/2 cup cornstarch

1/4 teaspoon salt

4 large eggs at room temperature, separated (yolks for filling, whites for meringue)

3 cups hot (but not scalding) whole milk

1 teaspoon vanilla

3/4 cup flaked coconut*

Meringue

4 egg whites

1/4 teaspoon cream of tartar

1/3 cup sugar

1/4 cup flaked coconut

1. For the pie crust, combine the flour and salt in a large mixing bowl. Add the shortening, and break it up into the flour with a pastry blender or fork until you get a crumbly mixture. This can be done in a food processor. But in either case, don't overmix.

2. Add 4 tablespoons of the ice water, and mix until the dough just comes together. If it is still crumbly, add more water, 1 tablespoon at a time. The dough should be slightly sticky. (Add a bit more flour if it is too sticky.) Form into a ball, cover with plastic wrap, and refrigerate at least 30 minutes.

3. Meanwhile, make the filling. Put just enough water in the bottom of a double boiler or a saucepan large enough to hold a medium-large, heatproof mixing bowl so that the water doesn't touch the top of the double boiler** or the heatproof bowl. Heat the water until it simmers.

4. While the water heats, gently whisk the sugar, cornstarch, and salt in a heatproof bowl or the top of a double boiler. Add the egg yolks, one at a time, and mix well. While whisking the egg yolk mixture constantly, very gradually dribble in about a cup of the hot milk. Add the second cup a little faster, again while whisking constantly. Then add the third cup.

5. Place the bowl over simmering water, and stir the ingredients until it thickens, about 20 minutes. When cooked, add the vanilla and 3/4 cup of coconut. Set aside to cool until the pie crust is done.

6. Heat the oven to 375 degrees. Place the dough on a floured flat surface. Roll out the dough wide enough to line a 9-inch pie plate. Place dough over the pie plate, and fit in

the dough using your lightly dusted fingers. Prick the sides and bottom with a fork. To flute the edges, see Tucking and Pinching Pie Dough, below.

7. Bake for about 30 minutes or until lightly brown. Remove to cool slightly while you make the meringue. Keep the oven on.

8. Beat the egg whites with cream of tartar. Gradually add sugar, and beat until stiff and almost dry.

9. Pour the filling into the pie crust. Spread the meringue on top, swirling a bit to create small peaks. Sprinkle with remaining 1/4 cup of coconut.

10. Bake until the meringue and coconut are lightly brown, 10 to 12 minutes. Serve slightly cool. Makes 6 servings.

* Recipe Note: You can buy coconut hermetically sealed in a can, or you (and your kids) can have some fun and buy a fresh coconut, like we used to do. Poke a few holes in the "eyes," and drain the liquid. It's delicious. Then crack the shell and dig out the meat. Peel the skin off for this recipe. Then grate the coconut pieces on the medium-size holes of a box grater. (For eating out of hand, don't bother peeling.)

** I've used the double boiler that Mom used, but I prefer a bowl over a pot of simmering water because the rounder bowl allows me to get at all the filling more easily.

Tucking and Pinching Pie Dough

After fitting the dough in a pie plate, lift the dough that's hanging over the side of the pie plate, and gently tuck it under, so you have a rolled edge. Dip your fingertips in flour periodically to prevent sticking.

The next step is the "pinch." Point the index finger of your left hand down (assuming you're right-handed), on the outside edge of the pie shell. Place the thumb and index finger of your right hand about an inch apart, on the inside edge of the pie shell. Push the edge of the dough with the side of your left index finger into the opening made by your right thumb and index finger, and pinch slightly with your right hand as you do this. This will make a wave-like pattern all around the edge of the pie shell. Again, flour your fingertips to prevent sticking.

When making a double-crust pie, like peach or apple, you reverse the "lift-and-tuck" step. After rolling out and placing the bottom crust in the pie plate and adding the filling, lay the top crust over the filling so it just barely reaches the edges of the plate. Roll the bottom crust over the top and curl upward. This reverse "lift-and-tuck" method prevents leakage. Then proceed with the pinch step.

LEMON MERINGUE PIE

Pie Crust

See ingredients and method
   for Coconut Cream Pie

Filling

1 1/2 boxes lemon pudding
   and pie filling*

3/4 cup sugar

3 1/3 cups water

3 eggs, separated (yolks for
   filling, whites for meringue)

Meringue

See ingredients and method
   for Coconut Cream Pie.

1. Make, bake, and cool the pie crust as in Coconut Cream Pie.

2. Make filling according to package instructions. Pour into the pie crust and smooth out the filling. Refrigerate until the meringue is done.

3. Make the meringue, as in step 8 for Coconut Cream Pie. Spread atop the filling, and bake, as in step 10 for Coconut Cream Pie.

4. Chill until ready to serve. Makes 6 servings.

* Recipe Note: Do not use instant pie fillings. They do not require eggs, which you need for the meringue. They also contain a lot of chemicals that you certainly don't need.

LITTLE LEFTOVER PIECES OF DOUGH FROM PIES

You should eat these pieces as soon as they come out of the oven. Unlike the pies, they are not nearly as good when cooled.

Leftover dough from pies

Sugar

Cinnamon

1. Heat the oven to 400 degrees. Meanwhile, gather any scraps of excess dough from pies and shape into a ball. Roll out the dough to the thickness of a pie crust, or about 1/8 inch. (Don't worry about the shape.)

2. Put rolled out dough on a cookie sheet. Sprinkle with sugar and dust lightly with cinnamon. Cut into pieces, about 2 inches by 2 inches or so. (Don't fret about uniformity.)

3. Bake until crisp, about 15 minutes. Serve at once.

RICE PUDDING

This is a recipe that Mom got from Dad's stepmother, who taught Mom more about cooking than her own mother did. It's delicious and easy to prepare.

1 cup long-grain white rice

1 1/8 teaspoons salt, divided

2 cups whole milk

3/4 cup raisins

1 egg

1/2 cup sugar

1/4 teaspoon nutmeg (or to taste)

1/2 teaspoon cinnamon (or to taste), plus more for garnish

1. Put the rice in a medium saucepan with 1 teaspoon of the salt and 2 cups of water. Bring to a boil, reduce to a simmer, and cook, covered, for 10 minutes. Turn off the heat, and let the rice steam (covered) until done (when the water is gone and holes dot the surface of the rice).

2. While the rice is cooking, put just enough water in the bottom of a double boiler or a saucepan large enough to hold a medium-large, heatproof mixing bowl so that the water doesn't touch the top of the double boiler or the heatproof bowl. Heat the water until it simmers. Add the milk and raisins to the top of a double boiler or the bowl and cook for 15 minutes, stirring periodically.

3. Add the cooked rice to the milk, and heat 5 minutes, stirring a few times. While the rice is heating, mix the egg with the sugar and 1/4 teaspoon of salt in a small bowl. Add nutmeg and cinnamon to taste.

4. Add a few tablespoons of the hot milk and rice to the egg mixture, and combine well. Mix in a few more tablespoons of hot milk and rice. (This will prevent the eggs from curdling.) Add the egg mixture to the rice, and stir frequently while cooking for 3 minutes.

5. Pour the rice pudding into a shallow serving container. Allow to cool at room temperature, then refrigerate until ready to serve. Dust with cinnamon before serving. Serves 4–6.

WITHOUT BREAD

Mom gave us lots of rules to live by. Because we were obedient and respectful children, we followed these rules as if forged in cast iron. We also knew that Mom was never far away from her favorite instrument of discipline, a three-foot wooden spoon she used alternately to stir spaghetti sauce and whack our behinds.

Many of these rules might be categorized as old wives' tales. We were instructed to put butter on a burn. And we were warned not to play with our food, among other things. One of the more curious rules was an admonition against walking around the house barefooted because we might step on a nail. Where these nails were to come from, we were never told.

Once Mom saw a public service announcement on television, warning about the dangers of swimming immediately after a full meal. Unfortunately, Mom took this rule to include merely going into any water, so she forbade us from taking a bath or shower until at least two hours had passed after we ate.

Another rule of Mom's—and many other mothers—was "Don't eat that; you'll spoil your dinner." Regardless of what "that" was, it didn't completely excuse you from dinner, not that we really wanted to be excused. (Actually, Russ was always excusing himself. Frank and I often had to pitch in and help him eat his vegetables. But what are brothers for, anyway?)

If we happened to violate that rule, Mom was ready with another. It didn't matter what we were having for dinner. It could be lasagna with meatballs and braciola, roasted chicken with potatoes and onions, or lamb stew. Too much food? Eat it without bread.

According to Mom, eating anything without bread was going to make it seem like a canapé at a garden party. The pounds of protein and fat didn't matter. Eating without bread was practically dieting. We did eat bread with most meals, though it wasn't that cottony "American" bread that was good only for peanut butter and jelly sandwiches (which we rarely ate). We ate Italian bread.

Mom would make a cross with the knife on the bottom of the loaf before she cut it. This was either a religious act or insurance against a substandard loaf. She gave us the middle slices, implying that by keeping the ends for herself, she was doing us a favor.

After I left home, I discovered that the best pieces were the ends. That's OK, Mom; we still love you.

Bread was not just for eating. For Mom, it conveyed a certain sense of wanting or needing. For example, if someone had a mop of unruly hair on his head, Mom would say, "He needs a haircut like the bread."

We ate bread with every meal except when we ate spaghetti or some other kind of pasta. That made sense to me. Why would you eat starch with another starch? When I was off on my own after college, I noticed that some people ate bread with their pasta. I thought, *These people must be* really *hungry.*

Dad was often the rule enforcer for Mom—"Do what your mother tells you!" And while eating without bread was Mom's suggestion when we *weren't* especially hungry, Dad was ready with one of his own rules if we *were.* If we were still hungry after a meal, Dad would bark, "Hungry? Eat bread."

Then, as if to dare us to be hungry after consuming mass quantities of bread, Dad would smile and say, "And if you're still hungry after that, eat this." He would then thrust out his forearm as an offering. We got the message. Dad's forearm was the size of a fire hydrant and just as impenetrable.

We used to have freshly baked bread frequently when we lived upstairs from my grandmother. (Nobody called it a "duplex" in those days. In Buffalo, it was just a two-family house.) Grandma always had food ready when we stopped by. Food was her way of communicating since she spoke virtually no English, and her grandchildren spoke an equal amount of Italian. Her first words upon greeting us were not an Italian version of "So good to see you" or "Here are my wonderful grandchildren." Instead, Grandma greeted us with a simple question: "*Mangaste*?" or "Have you eaten?" (Like all my relatives, Grandma spoke in a Sicilian dialect that defies even the tentacles of Google, which lists "Hai mangiato?" as "Have you eaten?" in Italian.)

Grandma's bread was a delicious stubby loaf with toasted sesame seeds on top. We ate it while it was still warm because the enticing aroma found us wherever we were. Soon, we were tearing at it to eat with ham, cheese, butter, or just by itself. The poor loaf never got a chance to cool.

I'm going to give you a recipe for a kind of bread Grandma used to make for holidays. Actually, it's not really bread but what my wife, Mary, calls a "bread product," meaning anything made with baked dough (which includes pizza, bagels, etc.) The derivation and spelling of *billulata*, as with so many family recipes, is mysterious. People like Grandma didn't write things down. They kept them in their heads and verbalized them in their own dialect.

Grandma brought the recipe with her from Sicily. After she died in 1967, Mom baked billulata well into her 80s. Like Grandma, Mom made billulata only on holidays, which is when they made it in Sicily because meat was expensive. The holiday tradition continued into the new world, even though meat became much more plentiful and cheaper. And because two of my siblings and I lived in other cities, Mom also considered our infrequent visits to be holidays as well.

When she knew we were coming home for a visit, she would bake a few recipes of billulata ahead of time. She put them in the freezer alongside containers of tripe and sausage so we could help ourselves before we left—and take whatever we could manage on the plane. Mom made a pretty fair sausage, incidentally. It tastes great on a fresh roll. (See Mom's Sausage recipe, Picnic chapter.) Sometimes, though, I'm just not that hungry. Then I'll eat it without bread.

Grandma, Sam, and Frank

From left: Little Aunt Jo, Mom, and Aunt Betty with
seven of their (eventual) eleven children

BILLULATA

Billulata was typically served on holidays as part of a kind of buffet with olive salad, sausage, pizza, and whatever else Mom decided. The number of servings varied. Figure the four loaves will serve between 12 and 16 people

Dough

7 cups all-purpose flour

4 tablespoons shortening at room temperature

1 egg at room temperature

1 tablespoon sugar

1 tablespoon salt

1 package dry yeast

Warm water (100 to 110 degrees), about 2 cups

2 tablespoons olive oil

Filling

4 1/2 pounds ground beef

Salt and pepper to taste

4 pounds onions, thinly sliced

8 tablespoons (1/2 cup) olive oil, divided

1 1/3 cups Parmigiano cheese

Topping

1 egg, beaten

1/3 cup sesame seeds

1. Place the flour in a large mixing bowl or on a large flat working surface. Make a well in the center. In a small bowl, combine the shortening, egg, sugar, salt, and yeast. Add this mixture to the well. Stir in 1/2 cup of the warm water, and let sit a few minutes for the yeast to dissolve. Gradually incorporate the yeast mixture into the flour. Add just enough warm water to make an elastic, slightly sticky dough. Let the dough sit for 10 minutes. It will not be smooth at this point.

2. In the bottom of a clean bowl or large pot, add 1 tablespoon of olive oil. Add the dough, and knead until smooth. With the smooth, bottom side of the dough facing up, cover the bowl with a dish towel and place in a draft-free warm area for 1 1/2 hours or until volume of the dough is approximately doubled.

3. The filling will need to be cooked in stages. (Unless you have a very large frying pan, this will go faster if you use two frying pans.) Cook the beef until it loses color. With a slotted spoon to drain the fat, put the beef into a large bowl. Season with salt and pepper.

4. Pour out any fat from the frying pans, and add one tablespoon oil to each. (If you are using one large pan, add two tablespoons to that pan.) Sauté 1/4 of the onions until soft and lightly browned. Add the onion to the bowl with the beef. Repeat until all the onion is cooked. (Don't overload the pan(s) with onions in an effort to reduce the number of batches. This will result in steamed, not sauteed onions.) Mix the onion and beef well. Adjust for salt and pepper as needed. Refrigerate.

5. With a fist, punch down the dough to deflate it. Knead for a minute or two, and cover. Let sit for 1 1/2 hours or until volume has approximately doubled.

6. Remove the beef and onion mixture from the refrigerator. Punch down the dough and cut into 4 pieces of equal size. Roll out each into a rectangle approximately 10 x 16 inches. Have the longer side of each rectangle running horizontally as you begin the filling and rolling. Lightly brush each with a tablespoon of the remaining olive oil from the dough ingredient list. Spread 1/4 of the filling evenly on each rectangle, leaving 1 inch around the edges uncovered. Sprinkle on 1/3 cup of the cheese.

7. Roll up the dough as you would a jelly roll, starting with the longer horizontal side nearest to you. Roll the dough about halfway, then fold in the ends and continue rolling. Seal the ends and top with water. Put on cookie sheets (you may need two cookie sheets for the four loaves) with the sealed flaps underneath. Repeat with the next three loaves. Allow 1–2 inches between loaves for expansion. Cover, and let rise for 1 hour.

8. Heat the oven to 385 degrees. Brush each loaf with 1/4 of the beaten egg and sprinkle each with 1/4 of the sesame seeds.

9. If your oven is big enough, bake both sheets in the lower third of the oven for 20 minutes. (Otherwise, do one at a time.) Bake in upper third of the oven for 10 minutes or until lightly browned. Let cool slightly before serving. I think it's best warm or at room temperature. Yield 4 loaves.

CHICKEN CACCIATORE

Chicken cacciatore has nothing to do with bread-making, but it does have something to do with bread. It is one of those dishes (snails and tripe being two others that come to mind) that cry out for bread. The bread, of course, is for dunking in the sauce. Mom suggested you have a "nice salad" with this dish to make this a complete meal.

The recipe originated with my aunt Jo, or big Aunt Jo, as she was frequently called, to distinguish her from Little Aunt Jo. This had nothing to do with their size. It was a consequence of who they married. Big Aunt Jo (nee Josephine) was married to Mom's oldest brother, Uncle Alphonso (aka Big Al). Little Aunt Jo was married to Mom's youngest brother, Uncle Albert, known as Little Al.

Albert was not his birth name, however. It was Balthazar, not a name that would make it easy for a kid to assimilate into the American melting pot. So my grandparents changed it to something more American. Why they changed it to Albert, a name so close to their oldest son's name, Alphonso, instead of Phil or Tony, I never found out.

Tony, by the way, is what my aunt Betty used to call my uncle Charlie. Uncle Charlie was quite the ladies' man when single. And he had a habit of giving women he dated different names for himself because few of these relationships lasted. Why give away your real name to someone you'd never see again? Aunt Betty, however, stuck. And so did the name Tony. Charlie's birth name, incidentally, was Colangelo.

Anyway, Mom made some modifications to Big Aunt Jo's recipe, primarily baking the chicken first, rather than frying, to reduce the fat. (Mom did this kind of thing more and more as she got older. But that didn't stop her from putting spareribs and ham hocks in the spaghetti sauce.) I also made a few modifications, mostly ratcheting up the seasonings.

2 frying chickens, cut into
   serving pieces

Salt and pepper to taste

Paprika

4 tablespoons olive oil

2 green bell peppers, chopped
   into 1/2-inch pieces

1 large onion, chopped

3 cloves garlic, finely chopped

1 pound mushrooms, sliced

1 quart Mom's Canned
   Tomatoes (see Can Do
   chapter) or 1 (28-ounce)
   can Italian plum tomatoes,
   seeded and chopped (retain
   juice)

1 (28-ounce) can tomato
   puree

2 tablespoons chopped fresh
   basil

2 teaspoons dried oregano

2 bay leaves

1. Heat the oven to 400 degrees. Season the chicken pieces to taste with salt, pepper, and paprika. Put the pieces on a rack over a sheet pan. Bake in the oven for 30 minutes, turning over once. Remove, and set aside.

2. While the chicken is baking, heat 2 tablespoons of the oil in a large skillet. Sauté the peppers over medium-high heat. When the peppers just begin to soften, remove them with a slotted spoon to a 4-quart saucepan or Dutch oven. Add the onion to the skillet, cook a few minutes, then add the garlic. Cook until the onion is translucent. Add to the saucepan.

3. Put the remaining 2 tablespoons of oil in the skillet, and sauté the mushrooms. When they are lightly browned, add them to the saucepan. (Unless your skillet is sufficiently large, you may have to do the mushrooms in two batches. Otherwise, they would be steamed instead of sauteed.)

4. Add the tomatoes and juice to the vegetables. Add the tomato puree. Rinse out the puree can with a little water, and add to the saucepan. Add the remaining ingredients, and simmer for 30 minutes.

5. Heat the oven to 350 degrees.

6. Put one cup of the sauce in the bottom of a roasting pan or casserole dish large enough to hold all the chicken and sauce. Layer half the chicken on the sauce. Repeat, making sure the top layer of chicken is covered with sauce.

7. Cover and bake for 30 to 35 minutes. Serve with rice or noodles. Serves 6–8.

ETHNIC EXOTICA

I wasn't always comfortable with being Italian. Actually, I'm Sicilian, which, for better or worse, has a special meaning for Italians and non-Italians alike. When I tell people I'm Sicilian, they have a tendency to raise their eyebrows and say, "Ah, Sicilian." Others, like Annie, the dishwasher I inherited when I took over Vincenzo's, my first restaurant, made comments about how Sicilians were always carrying knives.

Two films, *The Godfather* and *Swept Away*, helped me to realize that it was OK, if not downright cool, to be Italian and especially Sicilian. *Swept Away* is the story of how a macho Sicilian sailor dominates an aristocratic northern Italian female while they are marooned on an island together after a shipwreck. After seeing the film, a woman I worked with came up to me and said, "Hey, Sam, I understand you're Sicilian."

"Yes, both sides of the family, as a matter of fact."

"What are you doing tonight?"

As I said, I haven't always felt that way. When I was growing up, I felt self-conscious about being different. For instance, I was always taller than everyone in my class at school. You can't blame that on being Sicilian, of course. But some people thought it odd because Sicilians are supposed to be short. (At nearly six feet four inches, I used to call myself the world's tallest Sicilian.)

My family didn't look anything like the sitcom families on television. We were a decade or so away from the Kojaks, Banaceks, and Colombos. My father looked more like Archie Bunker from *All in the Family* than Robert Young from *Father Knows Best*. I remember wanting to change my name because I thought it sounded funny and because people were always mispronouncing it—goo-GHEEN-oh or jew-GHEEN-oh, or jew-JEAN-oh—instead of goo-JEAN-oh.

(Dad would sometimes give non-Italians a little pronunciation lesson, which didn't always make things easier for them. "Can you say 'goo'? Can you say 'JEEN'? Can you say 'oh'? Now put them all together.")

Nowhere was our ethnicity more evident than in the food we ate. How many kids do you think were weaned on tripe and spaghetti sauce with ham hocks and pig tails, as well as artichokes, snails, and dandelions? We didn't even eat the right kind of pizza. My mother always made what has now become popularized as "Sicilian-style" pizza. Back then, thick pizza was about as common as Beaujolais Nouveau.

There may be some people in the hinterlands who think the artichoke is a wrestling hold, but artichokes are certainly much more widely known today than they were in the 1950s and '60s. Mom prepared artichokes as part of a meatless smorgasbord on Fridays. Though I loved artichokes, I tried not to let it get around the neighborhood that, once a week, I scraped off the leaves of a strange plant with my teeth as part of my dinner.

Despite the artichoke's widespread availability today, there are still people who don't know how to eat a fresh one. Once, Mary and I were giving a dinner party, with artichokes as the first course. When we brought the plates back to the kitchen, we noticed that one person, who had either never eaten an artichoke before or loved them more than we could imagine, ate the whole thing, tough outer leaves, thistle, and all. Either that, or she stuffed the leaves in her purse. I've given directions for how to eat an artichoke in the Artichokes a la Grecque recipe in this chapter. If you're still feeling a bit intimidated, you might want to consult a YouTube video or wait to see how others at the table are eating their artichokes and follow suit.

The artichoke is a versatile vegetable that can be stuffed, dipped, or eaten by itself. I've stuffed them with sausage, ricotta, and seviche—not all together, though. Mom stuffed them with onions. Big Aunt Jo stuffed them with bread crumbs, which I preferred, though I never told Mom that. For a refreshingly different low-cal appetizer, eat them without any accompaniment, as in Artichokes a la Grecque. Or dip the edible ends of the artichoke leaves in a vinaigrette, hollandaise, or mayonnaise.

Of all the foods we ate, none was more exotic than cardoons, also called *cardoni* or *cardi*. In addition to picking her own dandelions, Mom also picked cardoons. But instead of digging them out of our front lawn, Mom found cardoons growing around railroad stops. This made them all the more mysterious. When I asked Mom why they grew in those locales, she told me that cattle cars would stop there for refueling. The floors were slatted, and, well, you get the picture.

The cardoon is a thistle related to the artichoke. Sometimes it's even referred to as the artichoke thistle. But it looks nothing like an artichoke. It looks more like a pale head of celery. Though the wild cardoons Mom harvested were slightly smaller than celery, cultivated cardoons look like celery after weight training.

While the artichoke has become more well known, the cardoon remains an obscure vegetable, even to many Italian Americans. Yet according to *The Oxford Companion to Food*, "Long before the artichoke was developed, the ancient Greeks and Romans regarded the cardoon as a great delicacy."

Cardoons are not easy to find, even in places you'd expect, like Italian American enclaves in major cities. They are primarily grown in California, much like most of the domestic artichokes we consume. Their season typically runs from late November through early spring.

You might find cardoons in some restaurants (especially in California) that feature the cooking of Piedmont, the northwestern Italian region famous for Barbera, Barolo, and Barbaresco. Some Piedmontese eat them raw (after peeling them like celery) with a delicious hot anchovy dip called bagna cauda, which I served with crudités in my first restaurant, Vincenzo's.

I can't imagine the cardoons eaten raw. Regardless of the final preparation, Mom always blanched cardoons first to remove some of the bitterness. Most commonly we ate cardoons in omelets or breaded, then fried. Both were staples on Fridays and during Lent.

ARTICHOKES A LA GRECQUE

This recipe is from my first cookbook, *Eat Fresh, Stay Healthy* (Simon & Schuster). If you are watching your weight, this is a very low-cal appetizer.

3/4 teaspoon each, black peppercorns, coriander seeds, and fennel seeds

2 bay leaves

A few branches of fresh thyme or 1/2 teaspoon dried thyme

1 whole chili pepper or a pinch of red pepper flakes

3 cloves garlic, crushed

6 parsley stems

1 teaspoon salt

2 tablespoons extra-virgin olive oil

1 cup dry white wine or dry vermouth

4 medium or 2 large artichokes

1 lemon, washed thoroughly and halved

1. Wrap the first six ingredients in cheesecloth and tie. Put the cheesecloth in a 4-quart pot with the salt, olive oil, wine or vermouth, and 3 quarts of water. Bring to a boil and simmer for 10 minutes or more.

2. Meanwhile, cut off the artichoke stems. Peel the stems and remove about a quarter inch or so from the bottom. Set the stems aside. As you work, rub the cut portions of the artichokes with a cut lemon to prevent discoloration. Put the artichokes on their sides and cut about one inch off the tops of each artichoke. Remove the withered leaves at the base of the artichoke. Trim 1/2 inch or so from the tops of the other leaves with scissors.

3. Squeeze the juice from the lemon into the flavored water, and toss in the lemon halves. Add the artichokes and stems. Cover with a plate to keep submerged, and cook for about 25 minutes or until the base of the artichoke can easily be pierced with a knife.

4. Remove the artichokes, squeeze them gently to remove excess moisture, and set them aside upside down with the stems until cool enough to handle. Cut each artichoke in half, lengthwise. With a spoon, remove the fuzzy, prickly, and purplish "choke" from inside each artichoke half. A serving is half of a large artichoke or two halves of a medium one.

5. Eat the artichokes as is (warm or at room temperature), with or without a dip, such as mayonnaise or a vinaigrette. Start from the outside of the artichoke. Dip the meaty tip of each leaf into a dip, if using. Then scrape the meat off with your teeth. As you work your way to the center of the artichoke, the leaves will have meatier tips. The heart at the center, as well as the stem, should be eaten with a knife and fork. Serves 4.

BIG AUNT JO'S STUFFED ARTICHOKES

6 medium to large artichokes

1/4 cup lemon juice or white vinegar

2 cups breadcrumbs

1/4 cup grated Parmigiano or Romano cheese

2 cloves garlic, put through a press

2 tablespoons or more chopped parsley (Italian type preferred)

1 teaspoon dried oregano

2 tablespoons fresh chopped basil or mint

Salt and pepper to taste

1/2 cup olive oil

6 fresh plum tomatoes, peeled, seeded, and chopped (or canned)

1 cup chicken stock

1/2 cup dry white wine or dry vermouth

1. Trim the artichokes, as in step 2 of Artichokes a la Grecque. Pry open the centers, and remove the fuzzy, prickly, and purplish chokes with a spoon. Place the artichokes in cold water with a few tablespoons of lemon juice or vinegar.

2. Chop the artichoke stems, and, in a bowl, combine them with the bread crumbs, cheese, garlic, parsley, oregano, basil or mint, salt and pepper, and 1/4 cup of the olive oil.

3. Heat the oven to 350 degrees. Remove the artichokes from the lemon water. Drain them thoroughly by squeezing them upside down. Spread open the centers and stuff with the bread crumb mixture. Spread apart outer leaves and put additional stuffing in between them.

4. Season the tomatoes with salt and pepper, and top each artichoke with them. Drizzle the remaining olive oil on top.

5. Put the artichokes in a covered roasting pan or casserole dish with the chicken stock and wine. Bake for 1 hour, removing the cover for the last 10 minutes. Serves 6.

Cardoons

FRIED CARDOONS

Once you've trimmed and blanched the cardoons, as in steps 1 and 2 below, you can put them in omelets. (See Vegetable Omelet recipe, page 106)

1 teaspoon salt plus more to taste

1 pound cardoons

1/2 cup lemon juice (bottled is fine)

1 2/3 cup bread crumbs

1/3 cup grated Parmigiano cheese

1 teaspoon dried oregano

2 tablespoons finely chopped mint

Pepper to taste

3 eggs, well beaten

Vegetable oil for frying

1. Bring 4 quarts of water to a boil. Add a teaspoon of salt.

2. Meanwhile, clean the cardoons by cutting off the base of the stalk and removing any damaged or dried-out ribs. With a paring knife, peel the outer edge of each rib as you would celery to remove some of the stringiness. (You don't have to be meticulous.) Cut cardoon ribs into 4- x 1-inch pieces. As you do, put the pieces in a bowl of cold water with the lemon juice.

3. When the water boils, add the cardoons, and boil gently for 15 minutes or more, until the cardoons are just tender but still firm. Drain, and set aside to cool.

4. Combine the bread crumbs, grated Parmigiano, oregano, and mint in a shallow bowl or soup plate. Season with salt and pepper. Put the eggs in another shallow bowl or soup plate, and season with salt and pepper.

5. Dip the cardoons in the beaten eggs, then in the bread crumb mixture. Put breaded cardoons on a waxed paper–lined platter or sheet pan, and refrigerate for 15–20 minutes to let the breading set.

6. Put a large skillet over medium-high heat. Add the oil to a depth of 1 inch. When the oil is hot, add the cardoons. Cook until golden brown on both sides. Don't crowd the pan. Drain on paper towels. Keep cooked cardoons warm in a low-temperature oven until all are cooked. Serve at once. Serves 2–4 as a side dish.

THERE'S NO PLACE LIKE HOME FOR THE HOLIDAYS

When eating is the focal point in family life, holidays like Thanksgiving and Christmas are especially important. That's because we get to eat more than usual, which, under ordinary circumstances, may border on the prodigious. It's almost considered impolite not to stuff yourself to the point of oblivion. I guess it's like belching in Arabic countries to show how much you enjoyed your host's food.

Italians, even when they're eating something "American," like turkey, take a back seat to no one when it comes to volume. My former butcher, Sonny D'Angelo, irascible and ill-humored even to his regular customers, explained it very simply: "If I'm buying a roast or goose, and I'm trying to figure out how many it will serve, I ask, 'Are they Italian?'" He then gives the breakdown of servings for Italians and non-Italians, the latter eating somewhere around 50 percent less.

Here's an example. One of our friends is a WASP through and through. When her mother put your plate of food in front of you, that's all the food you were going to get. And it wasn't that much to begin with. Once, while staying at her mother's house for a few days, we were sipping coffee and juice in preparation for going out to eat a real breakfast. In an effort to be helpful, the mother opened the refrigerator door and said, "I think there's half an English muffin in here somewhere." Half an English muffin? Mom would split a side laughing.

Though the French invented it, I think WASPs must have been the ones to promote nouvelle cuisine with its microscopic portions. It's beautiful, but you can't eat a picture. Someone once said you can never be too thin. Obviously, not an Italian.

Contrary to what some may think, we do have the traditional turkey at Thanksgiving, and, no, we don't stuff it with ravioli. We did have lots of turkey, though. How much turkey? Generally, Mom cooked two 23-pounders. Forty-six pounds of turkey! God forbid that any nook of your body should be deprived of a turkey molecule. And, of course, a little left over for nibbling any time of the day or night.

Even if turkeys came in 50-pound sizes, Mom would still get two turkeys because she needed the extra drumsticks. My brothers and I wouldn't think of turkey without them, so right away, there's three. My cousins argued over the fourth, but some of them actually asked for white meat. Can you imagine?

To this day, I know that (a) I will always cook more food than I need for my guests, and (b) whatever is left over will be consumed before I go to bed, or I'll find a reason to get up in the middle of the night to eat it. We're talking heavy-duty, early oral conditioning here.

All my aunts (well, most of them) were pretty good cooks, but Mom, without anybody really saying it, was the best. Consequently, more often than not, relatives came to our house for the holidays. In fact, they came to our house all year long. We were the family version of the all-night diner. We never closed, even on holidays—especially on holidays.

I was, and still am, especially fond of Mom's bread stuffing. It is so very simple yet so delicious, despite the fact she used white bread and margarine. Mom would make it the night before, enough to fill a queen-size mattress. Of course, we ate half of it before it had a chance to cool. Now that was real comfort food.

There were always two tables set for the holiday meal, the adult table and the kids' table. It was a sign of status when you were old enough to eat with the adults. Until then it was with the other kids on card tables in the living room.

Though Mom's Thanksgiving meals were good, they were pretty conventional and didn't change much: turkey, gravy, sweet potatoes, mashed potatoes, cranberry sauce, broccoli, carrots, and salad.

When I got older and involved in the food business, I craved some variety. I love traditional Thanksgiving foods. But I like them best when they are prepared in non-traditional ways, with ingredients like coconut milk, persimmons, and pomegranate seeds.

Cranberries are a good example. Mom, a scratch cook with many dishes, never made fresh cranberry sauce. We always had that molded cranberry gelatin right from the can. It reminded me of a maroon slinky. Yet sauce made from fresh cranberries is as easy as pie—easier than pie—and lends itself to so many variations, some of which I've listed in the recipe section.

The eating didn't end with the turkey dinner. No siree. After a nice, light dessert of pumpkin pie with whipped cream or a coconut cream pie that could sink a battleship, the table was cleared for fresh fruit and roasted nuts in the shell. If you weren't snoozing in front of the television, you were popping almonds or filberts (the old-fashioned name we used for hazelnuts). Then there were a few hands of pinochle, and before you knew it, it was time for another meal. Bring on the Genoa salami, capicola, provolone, olive salad, sausage, pepperoni, tomatoes, and pepperoncini. How about some cold turkey?

Football was always a big part of Thanksgiving. The Detroit Lions traditionally played the Green Bay Packers on television. For several years, we ate while watching the game. Then we got sophisticated (actually, Mom put her foot down) and timed dinner to start at the very instant the first half ended.

For many years, the public high school football championship game was played on Thanksgiving Day in Buffalo. My brother Russell and I played on a Riverside High School team that was good enough to appear in the championship game every year we were there. Frank went to Hutch Tech because he wanted to be an engineer. As luck would have it, one year we wound up playing against each other for the championship.

My father was faced with a dilemma, albeit an enviable one for most parents. Which side of the field was he going to sit on? President Kennedy had a similar problem when he attended the Army–Navy game a few years earlier. Kennedy was a navy man, but he was also a politician who didn't want to offend army supporters. He wound up spending half of the game on each side. Dad was a navy man, too, but that had no bearing on his decision. He reckoned that, since my team was heavily favored (we didn't lose a game in four years), Frank's team needed all the support it could get. And he was right. My school won 19–0, despite Frank's outstanding play at defensive end.

Russ and I took our time getting home, savoring the victory. Frank was already there. As we entered the door, Mom was waiting for us at the top of the stairs. "Shut up," she said before we could utter a syllable. "Don't say a word. Sit down, and enjoy your dinner." If we had any intentions of rubbing it in to Frank, they were instantly smothered.

Things have changed somewhat in the past twenty years or so. The Dallas Cowboys host the game, not the Lions or Packers. The high school league we were in was dissolved, and the teams in it were put in a larger league that included suburban schools. Though Russ remained in the Buffalo area, Frank, Maria, and I are spread out along the South and East, so it became harder for all of us to get together at the same time. Then Mom got into her 90s and couldn't manage Thanksgiving dinner. She died in 2013.

But there are always memories and recipes. Here are Mom's recipes for bread stuffing and pumpkin pie. I've also included some recipes for cranberry sauce, just in case you decide not to have a maroon slinky with your turkey.

MOM'S BREAD STUFFING

This is best done a day ahead—if you can keep your hands away from it until dinner—because you want the turkey and the stuffing at room temperature when the turkey is stuffed. Though I think the dressing tastes best when flavored with the turkey juices during roasting, the Spanek roasting recipe below only allows for a small cavity above the breast to be stuffed. That's for you, if you're cooking the bird, and maybe your current best friend, if you're being generous.

2–3 cups warm water

2 pounds good-quality white bread, sliced

1/2 pound butter, approximately

5 ribs celery, cut into 1/4-inch-wide crescents

4 medium onions, finely chopped

2 tablespoons or more chopped fresh sage leaves

Salt and pepper to taste

1. Put the warm water in a bowl. Lightly dip each slice of bread in and squeeze out excess moisture. Crumble into a large mixing bowl (or chop very coarsely).

2. Put a large heavy-bottom skillet over medium heat. Add 2–3 tablespoons of butter. When the foam subsides, sauté the celery. When just tender, but not browned, remove the celery with a slotted spoon, and add it to the bread.

3. Add another tablespoon of butter to the pan, and sauté the onions until translucent. (Do this in two steps so as not to crowd the pan, which would steam the onions, not sauté them.) Add the onions to the bread.

4. Season the bread mixture with 2 tablespoons of the sage and salt and pepper. Mix thoroughly. Taste and add more seasoning, if desired.

5. Put the same skillet used for the onions over medium-high heat. Add 3 tablespoons of the remaining butter. When it stops foaming, turn the heat to high, and add the stuffing in batches—two or three depending on the size of your skillet. Just enough so the stuffing easily fits into the pan. Fry until the bread is golden brown, turning it over constantly to brown evenly and avoid burning. (I use two wide spatulas.) Lower the heat slightly, if necessary. Repeat with more butter and stuffing until it is all cooked.

6. Remove the stuffing to a large pan or bowl to cool. Enough stuffing for a 12- to 15-pound turkey. You can stuff the entire turkey in the traditional manner. Or follow the instructions below for the Spanek Roasted Turkey in which only a small cavity is stuffed and the remainder baked.

Sam carving Spanek turkey in Mom's kitchen

SPANEK ROASTED TURKEY

Mom's turkey-roasting method was fine but conventional. I'd like to give you a recipe for cooking a turkey an entirely different way. Years ago, when I was food editor of the *San Jose Mercury News*, I wrote about the Spanek vertical roaster, a metal frame that looks like a rough approximation of the Eiffel Tower. In fact, Anna Spanek was a cook in Paris when she created it. But it didn't take off until her son Denis began to market it aggressively in the 1990s. (Turkey and chicken roasters are available at spanek.com)

The turkey, sans stuffing (except for a small amount in the neck cavity), sits upright on the roaster, legs forward and wings akimbo, as if it were about to do a strut. That's all there is to it. No trussing. No basting.

The metal frame conducts the heat so well that the turkey cooks inside and out simultaneously. This sears in juices. You'll notice that when you cook a turkey this way, there will be virtually no juices in the drip pan below, only a small amount of fat. The juices are in the bird, where they're supposed to be. This is especially important for that all-too-often dry breast meat.

Because the turkey cooks inside and out at the same time, the cooking time is shorter. With the Spanek vertical roaster, a 15-pound turkey takes 2 to 2 1/2 hours in the oven or on a kettle grill (versus 3 1/2 hours cooked conventionally in an oven and three hours lying down on the grill).

Cooking on the grill frees up valuable oven space for those umpteen side dishes we demand at Thanksgiving. Even when cooked in the oven, the Spanek roasted turkey will stay hot long enough when it's done to allow you to finish side dishes in the oven.

Unless you're a butcher, or a grandpa who's been doing it for decades, carving a turkey can look like a Thanksgiving version of *The Texas Chainsaw Massacre*. But carving a stand-up bird is much easier. The breast comes off easily in two large pieces. (In one cooking demo, Denis Spanek took the breast off with a carrot instead of a knife.) And the breast doesn't fall apart when you slice it because it has so much moisture in it.

One final benefit of cooking your turkey on a vertical roaster in a kettle grill: you can set it and forget it. Light the fire and put in the bird; then, weather permitting, go play nine holes of golf. (Sorry, it cooks too fast for a full round.) Or stay home and watch football on television. But NO PEEKING! Lift that lid, and the temperature in the grill plummets.

Here's how to grill your Thanksgiving turkey upright, step by step.

1. Place a 22-inch Weber-type kettle grill in a non-drafty location. (Wind can severely lower the grill temperature.) Remove the top grill grate. You won't need it. (The grill lid has to close securely without touching the turkey, a clearance of about 11 inches, so it's a good idea to check before you decide to use the grill.)

2. Line a deep-dish pizza pan or similar pan with foil. Or use a disposable foil pan. Spray the vertical roaster with vegetable spray. (Makes for easier cleanup.) Get your seasonings ready. You'll need about 1/4 cup of poultry seasoning or all-purpose seasoning mix, such as herbes de Provence. Or make your own with ingredients as simple as salt, pepper, and crumbled sage leaves. Also have a tablespoon of paprika ready.

   (When working with any kind of poultry, it's a good idea to have everything you need on the work area ahead of time. This prevents touching surfaces with hands contaminated by the raw bird, which can spread salmonella. Always wash your hands and work surfaces thoroughly with soapy water after working with raw poultry.)

3. Remove giblets from the inside of a 15-pound turkey. Cut off the tail (it will help to make the turkey sit lower in the pan). You can roast the tail with the turkey and eat it the way my father and brothers and I did. (See Traditions chapter.) Or use it with the giblets for gravy stock. (See recipe below.)

4. In a chimney starter or by whichever method you prefer, heat 60 charcoal briquettes until hot. Pile 30 briquettes each on the two sides of the bottom grill grate. (You can buy charcoal baskets that fit on the sides, which keeps the briquettes together and makes cleanup easier.)

5. While the briquettes are heating, rub the inside of the turkey with seasoning. I also like to slip seasonings and olive oil or butter under the skin. Spray the outside of the turkey with vegetable spray and rub on the seasoning. Sprinkle the outside of the turkey with paprika. Set the turkey on the Spanek roaster. The top of the roaster should pop through the neck cavity. Push the bird down until it does. Legs should be in front. Tuck wing tips under and back. No need to truss, though you could make sure the wings stay in place by attaching them to the side of the breast with short metal skewers or trussing needles (the ones you normally need to sew up the cavity of the bird).

   If you are stuffing the turkey neck cavity, don't fill it too tight. Secure the skin over the stuffing with one or two of those trussing needles. (This amount of stuffing will serve only about two people. Bake the remaining stuffing, moistened with turkey stock, for about 30 minutes in a 350-degree oven when you prepare the side dishes.)

6. Put the vertical turkey in its pan on the grill. Put the grill lid on securely. This is vitally important. Make sure all the vents, top and bottom, are wide open. Don't touch that lid for 2 hours and 15 minutes.

7. Remove the turkey and check for doneness with an instant-read thermometer. It should register 165 degrees in the thickest part of the thigh. (The temperature will rise 10–15 degrees as the turkey rests before carving.)

   If the turkey is not fully cooked, put it in a 400-degree oven until it reaches the appropriate temperature. Or put it back into the grill if the coals are still hot, adding a half dozen or so more briquettes to each side.

   Remove the turkey while still on the vertical roaster. Wrap loosely with foil, and let it rest at least 20 minutes and as long as 40 minutes in a place that's not cold or drafty.

Oven Method: Follow steps two and three while preheating the oven to 450 degrees. Cook 30 minutes at 450. Lower heat to 350, and cook 1 3/4 hours longer. Then follow step seven.

(Oven temperatures may vary, so roasting times given are approximate. It's always a good idea to check the actual temperature in your oven with a thermometer so that you can know exactly how the temperature inside the oven compares with the outside dial and adjust accordingly.)

Carving a vertical bird:

1. With the turkey still on the Spanek roaster, remove the neck cavity, if it is stuffed, by making a V-shaped cut just above the breast. (I use a boning knife, but you can also use a kitchen utility knife.) Remove the section that contains the stuffing. If the cavity is not stuffed, make a similar cut and remove the wishbone at the top of the breast.

2. Push one of the legs down and away from the body of the turkey while cutting through where they meet. Do the same with the other leg. Separate the drumsticks from the thighs.

3. Remove the wings where they connect to the body of the turkey.

4. Cut down one side of the breast bone, scraping along the side of the breast bone with the knife as you pull the breast meat from the body of the turkey. Remove the half breast and repeat with the other side.

5. Put each breast half on the cutting board, cut side down, and cut each into slices of desired thickness. Arrange the turkey on a serving platter and moisten with some hot turkey stock. (See on the following page.)

TURKEY GRAVY

If you make the stock a day or two ahead—and I recommend that you do—you can roast the turkey parts and vegetables, which will give them more flavor and the stock more color. I always buy extra parts, especially necks, because what you get from one turkey isn't enough.

For the Turkey Stock

Turkey wing tips

Tail and giblets from turkey
(except the liver)*

2–3 pounds of extra turkey
parts, like necks or gizzards

2 small carrots, cut into
1-inch pieces

2 ribs celery, cut into 1-inch
pieces

1 small to medium onion, cut
into 1-inch pieces

1/2 cup dry white wine

3 quarts chicken stock

A dozen or so black
peppercorns

2 sprigs of thyme or 1
teaspoon dried

1 bay leaf

4 parsley stems

Cheesecloth

For the Gravy

3 tablespoons butter

3 tablespoons flour

1/4 cup port, sherry, or
Madeira (optional)

Salt to taste

Browning sauce, such as
Gravy Master or Kitchen
Bouquet

1. Heat the oven to 450 degrees.

2. For the stock, pat all the turkey parts and giblets dry with paper towels. Refrigerate the liver. Cut the necks and any other parts into pieces no larger than 3 inches long. Put the turkey parts and vegetables in a roasting pan. Roast in the oven until well browned, stirring periodically, about 25 minutes.

3. Remove the roasting pan from the oven, and put over two burners on the stove. Turn the heat to high, and add the wine and 3 cups of the chicken stock. As the mixture comes to a boil, scrape the bottom of the pan with a wooden spoon or heatproof spatula to loosen the flavorful bits on the bottom.

4. Meanwhile, wrap and tie the peppercorns, thyme, bay leaf, and parsley stems in cheesecloth. Put the contents of the roasting pan into a pot large enough to hold all the ingredients. Add the remaining chicken stock and the seasonings in the cheesecloth. Bring to a boil, lower the heat, and skim off any foam that appears on the top. Simmer 2 1/2 to 3 hours. Strain through a fine mesh sieve. Reserve the meat. (You should have about a quart of stock.) Refrigerate the turkey parts. Let the stock cool at room temperature for an hour, then refrigerate. Remove the fat that forms at the top of the cold stock before using the stock for gravy.

5. When ready to make the gravy, heat the stock. Put 1 tablespoon of the butter in a heavy-bottom saucepan over medium heat. Add the liver and cook until just cooked through. Chop the liver along with the heart and gizzard. Add the remaining butter to the saucepan over medium

heat. When hot, add the flour and cook for a few minutes until the mixture becomes light brown, stirring frequently with a whisk. Add 2 cups of the hot stock and whisk thoroughly until the gravy comes to a boil. Add the port, sherry, or Madeira, if desired. Reduce the heat and simmer until the gravy thickens, stirring periodically, about 10 minutes. Add the giblets (liver, heart, and gizzard). Season with salt to taste. If you want a meatier gravy, you can add some of the meat from the neck or tail. Add a teaspoon or so of browning sauce if you want it darker.

6. If made ahead, reheat the gravy just before serving. Add any juices from the carved turkey. If the gravy is too thin, mix together a tablespoon each of softened butter and flour until the flour is fully incorporated. Add a teaspoonful at a time to the gravy. If the gravy is too thick, add more stock. Makes about 2 cups.

*Liver can add a strong, sometimes bitter taste to the stock. But it's fine when prepared for the gravy.

PUMPKIN PIE

Pie Crust

See Coconut Cream Pie recipe for making and rolling out the dough, page 70.

Filling

2 cups canned pumpkin (not pumpkin pie mix)

1/2 teaspoon salt

1 cup sugar

1/2 teaspoon each ground cinnamon, mace (or nutmeg), and ginger

1/4 teaspoon ground cloves

2 eggs (at room temperature)

1 cup milk

1 cup heavy cream

1/3 cup powdered sugar or to taste

1. Heat the oven to 450 degrees.

2. Mix together pumpkin, salt, sugar, and spices. Beat the eggs with milk and half the cream. Add to pumpkin, stirring until well blended. Pour the pumpkin filling into the dough-lined pie shell.

3. Bake in oven for 10 minutes. Reduce heat to 325 degrees, and bake 50 to 60 minutes or until the center becomes somewhat firm. Cool on a wire rack.

4. Whip the remaining cream, adding the powdered sugar to taste. Serve the pie topped with whipped cream.

CRANBERRY SAUCE

In its simplest form, scratch cranberry sauce is just cranberries (fresh or frozen) with sugar and water, cooked until the cranberries pop after five minutes of rapid simmering. You can add any of the ingredients below to make things more interesting. You can also jazz up canned cranberry sauce (not gelatin) with them.

Fruits: apples, pears, persimmons, quince, and both the rind and juice of oranges and lemons

Nuts (preferably toasted): walnuts, pecans, hazelnuts, and almonds

Spices: ginger, primarily, fresh or candied

Alcohol: bourbon, rum, amaretto, and orange liqueurs like triple sec or Grand Marnier

Preserves: orange marmalade, apricot, peach, and almost any berry (adjust other added sweeteners accordingly)

Sweeteners: brown sugar, maple syrup

CRANBERRY SAUCE WITH CANDIED GINGER

12-ounce package of fresh or frozen cranberries, washed and picked over for damaged or off-color fruit

1 cup water

1 cup sugar

1/4 cup candied ginger, finely chopped

1. Combine all ingredients in a heavy-bottom saucepan. Bring to a boil over medium-high heat. Reduce heat, and simmer briskly for 5 minutes, a few minutes more if the cranberries were frozen. Stir periodically.

2. Cool to room temperature, then refrigerate up to 5 days. Serves 4 to 6.

CRANBERRY SAUCE WITH BOURBON AND PECANS

12-ounce package fresh or frozen cranberries, washed and picked through

3/4 cup sugar

2/3 cup apricot preserves

1/3 cup good-quality bourbon

2 tablespoons julienned orange peel

1/2 cup toasted pecans, coarsely chopped

1. Combine all ingredients, except pecans, in a heavy-bottom saucepan. Bring to a boil over medium-high heat. Reduce heat, and simmer briskly for 5 minutes, a few minutes more if the cranberries were frozen. Stir periodically.

2. Fold in the pecans. Cool to room temperature, then refrigerate up to 5 days. Serves 4 to 6.

SCHOOL LUNCHES

In recent years, more focus has been put on what kids eat in school. Michelle Obama deserves some credit for that. But before Ms. Obama was born, my mother knew what to put in her children's Davy Crockett and Roy Rogers lunch boxes or my father's black-domed metal lunch bucket. When it came to preparing food, Mom was in her element. It didn't make any difference if it was Sunday dinner, picnics, a feast for 300 on St. Joseph's Day, or school lunches.

Lunches were especially important because, during the week, we never ate much for breakfast, though Mom tried her best. Even then, she knew (without the aid of any nutritionists or First Ladies) that breakfast was an important meal. Unfortunately, my brothers and I often stayed up late studying the night before, or we would get up earlier than usual to finish a term paper. We weren't in the mood for a big meal at 7:30 a.m., unlike Dad, who could consume mass quantities at any time of the day or night. (My sister was just a tyke during this period, but in her own time, she was equally averse to breakfast.)

Mom, who had been up since 5:30, would wake us up with a cheery, "It's ten minutes to seven, boys." Do you know how difficult it is to be cheery at ten minutes to seven when you're fifteen? As if that weren't enough, Mom would then ask us for our breakfast orders.

"What do you kids want for breakfast? Eggs? Bacon? Pancakes? French toast?"

"Coffee, Mom, just coffee."

"You can't have 'just coffee.' How about some tea and toast?"

"OK, OK, tea and toast—and coffee."

The reason I mention this is because it gives you an idea of how hungry we were by lunchtime. Some nutritionists and children's cookbook authors have suggested decorating your child's lunch box or paper bag with stickers and other cutesy things in an effort to entice them to eat. Mom didn't need such inducements. Even my brother Russell, who was finicky about vegetables, had no trouble with his luncheon appetite. We wanted food, real food, and lots of it.

I once saw a recipe in *The Lunch Box Book* by Annie Gilbar for Elliott's Chicken and Peanut Flowers. In the first place, *Elliott* was a nerdy name for a kid in those days. The guys I went to school with and ate lunch with were named Bob, Dave, Joe, Al, and Bill.

OK, there was an Emory. And I'll admit Emory is a nerdy name. But we allowed Emory to sit with us because he played in a rock band.

Anyway, the recipe for Elliott's sandwich calls for the bread to be cut into a flower shape with a cookie cutter. It's bad enough when you give your kid a name like Elliott to live with, but why do you have to compound the problem by giving him flower sandwiches?

Mom's lunches were always good, basic meals and as balanced as Simone Biles on that narrow wooden beam. We had sandwiches—as many as three, if we wanted them—or something equally substantial, like cold chicken; dessert, like Aunt Sandy's famous cookies or Mom's very good chocolate cake; and fruit, always fresh fruit. This was an age when the term *fiber* was unknown to the general public. Mom called it "roughage." I never really understood or asked what roughage meant, and Mom never volunteered, except to say that we needed it. I suppose in the back of my mind I thought I'd learn about it at the appropriate time, like my wedding night. "Sam, you're getting married tomorrow, so I think it's time we had a talk about roughage."

The only thing Mom didn't pack in our lunch was a beverage, so I bought a pint of milk in the cafeteria. I think in eight years of grade school and four years of high school I bought my lunch once, and I soon blocked it out of my memory. With rare exceptions, from first through eighth grades, we came home for lunch every day. That meant even more substantial meals, like ravioli or Mom's delicious chicken soup—the kind you could eat with a fork, years before Campbell's ever thought of it. Going home for lunch enabled me to develop an early addiction (since cured) for soap operas. Back then, *Guiding Light* and *Search for Tomorrow* were only fifteen minutes long. I could watch both and still make it back to school on time.

Though we generally ate sandwiches in high school, it was never peanut butter and jelly. Nor was it that ubiquitous entity known as *lunch meat*. Emory had lunch meat often. I once asked him what was in lunch meat. He said, "What do you mean, what's in it? It's lunch meat." He made it sound as if there were little animals called lunches grazing in pastures, waiting to be made into lunch meat.

I had the good stuff. Sometimes it was capicola (a spicy cured ham) or mortadella (a bologna infinitely superior to Oscar Mayer). Occasionally, it was a breaded veal cutlet, and often, it was Genoa salami. My good friend Joey Gerstel was crazy about Genoa salami. He could smell it as soon as I got on the bus.

"You got Genoa salami today?"

"Yeah."

"Wanna trade?"

"Whaddaya got?"

"Egg salad."

"Forget about it, Joey."

To me, Genoa salami was routine, like lunch meat was to Emory, or peanut butter and jelly was to the nerds. To Joe, it was manna from heaven. You see, Joey was Jewish, and there's not a lot of call for Genoa salami in Jewish families. Tongue, yes; Genoa, no. Sometimes when I had Genoa salami, Joey had roast beef. Mom never made roast beef sandwiches for us, probably because there was no beef left after dinner the night before. So when he offered to trade on those occasions, I readily accepted. I overlooked the fact that he had put ketchup on it.

Most of our sandwiches had mayonnaise on them. At least I thought it was mayonnaise. It was really Miracle Whip, which wasn't nearly as rich as mayonnaise. It wasn't until I started shopping for myself during my last year in college that I noticed the difference. Ever since tasting real mayonnaise, I've never gone back to Miracle Whip. (Today, I buy Duke's, which I think is the best mayo on the supermarket shelves.)

VEGETABLE OMELET (FRITTATA)

When I was growing up, I never would have thought of omelets—or frittatas, what Italian omelets are called today—for lunch. But after several trips to Spain, where slices of omelet (called a tortilla in Spain) are served as part of a tapas spread, I think having some of Mom's vegetable omelets for lunch would have been a great idea.

8 eggs

1/3 cup grated Parmigiano or Romano cheese

2 tablespoons chopped fresh mint or basil

1 teaspoon dried oregano

Salt and pepper to taste

2 cups cooked, coarsely chopped vegetables, such as cauliflower, cardoons, broccoli, or spinach*

1–2 tablespoons olive oil

1. Turn on the broiler, and put a 9-inch cast-iron or similar ovenproof skillet over medium-high heat.

2. Beat the eggs, cheese, and seasonings together. Add the vegetables, and combine well.

3. Put the oil in the skillet. When the oil is hot but not smoking, add the omelet mixture.

4. Reduce the heat to medium, and cook until the bottom is set and firm. When the sides and bottom of the omelet are set, run a heatproof rubber spatula around the edge of the omelet to make it easier to slip out of the skillet when cooked. Put the skillet under the broiler until the top is firm, a minute or two. Slide the cooked omelet out of the skillet and onto a plate. Serve warm or at room temperature. Serves 4, more if part of a mix of appetizers or tapas.

* If using spinach or any vegetable that retains a lot of moisture, make sure to squeeze out excess moisture before adding it to the omelet.

SNACKING

Mom often said, "My kids eat one meal a day. They start when they get up in the morning, and they finish when they go to bed." That wasn't entirely true, however. Sometimes, we ate in bed.

Eating in our family was as important as breathing and occurred with about as much regularity. Though our meals were rituals of mass consumption, they were not the only times we ate. Hence, Mom's quote.

Sometimes, snacking was in the form of an actual meal. Our holiday dinners, like Thanksgiving and Christmas, occurred in the early afternoon, about one or two o'clock. Though the amount of food we ate at those meals was sufficient to send bears into hibernation for the winter, it was, after all, only the second meal of the day. (Unlike school days when we got up early, we ate breakfast on weekends and holidays when we were allowed to sleep in.) Since we ate three meals on Thanksgiving, the third, in this case, was a slight concession to moderation. (Moderation and eating, like oil and water, tended not to mix well in my family.)

Our third meal on holidays was referred to as a snack, which Mom, for some inexplicable reason, called a "snick-snack." Mom would walk into the living room, where half of us were sleeping off dinner and the other half were playing cards, and ask—announce, really—"How about a little snick-snack?" A little snick-snack was everything left over from the midday blowout, plus anything else in the refrigerator, like cold cuts, pickled eggplant, and Mom's olive salad. Just enough to tide you over until breakfast.

No one said anything like, "Food? Again? We just ate." Listen, to stay in my family, you had to be in shape. Holidays were playoff time, when early conditioning paid off. I don't understand these people who say, "I had such a big lunch I didn't feel like dinner."

Though most Middle American families aspired to two-car status, we thought it was more important—and a heckuva lot cheaper—to be a two-refrigerator family. The second fridge was essential to good snacking because that is where many of the leftovers were stored. We also needed a second refrigerator because no model yet constructed, at least not one that could fit through the doorway, could hold all our weekly needs. (Though my current family is just my wife and me, we still have two refrigerators—and a freezer!)

In order to snack properly, you must have a sufficient quantity and variety of food. Mom was very obliging by always having both. It was no coincidence that Mom cashed

Dad's paycheck at the supermarket. Sometimes, Mom didn't have a chance to get the food home before we snacked. When we were young, Mom shopped at an old-fashioned butcher shop in our Italian neighborhood. It used to sell loose hot dogs and wrap them in butcher paper. No sooner did Mom bring the bags to the car than we were all diving in for those hot dogs to munch on until we got home for lunch.

Mom rarely bought junk food. Sure, we ate pretzels and potato chips, but not that often. Instead, she'd make her own popcorn. Mom had a pot used expressly for this purpose. She'd keep it on a shelf underneath the stairs to the second floor. This may be nostalgia talking, but somehow that popcorn tasted better than any popcorn I've made in a microwave oven.

Mostly, the kinds of things we snacked on were the kinds of food we would eat as a meal. For example, we always had cheese, pepperoni, olives, and pepperoncini peppers around the house. A common snack was a hunk of cheese, a piece of pepperoni, a few olives, a couple of pepperoncini, and some Italian bread. For us, this was as natural as a Twinkie was for other kids.

One of the few concessions to junk food was doughnuts. We'd often pick up a dozen on a summer's evening when we went with Dad to get the early edition of the *Courier Express*, Buffalo's morning newspaper, when the city, like so many others, had two newspapers or more. We ate the doughnuts and washed them down with coffee from the perpetual pot Mom maintained on the stove. It was never decaf, though that didn't seem to keep us awake at night.

A snack could be, and often was, a sandwich. It might be filled with some form of cold cut, like Genoa salami or capicola, or leftover meat, like turkey or meatballs. Sometimes, it could be a little more exotic, like Mom's canned eggplant. These thick slices were oozing with oil and spiked with hot pepper and garlic. Messy, but delicious.

(Mom called a sandwich a "sangwich," like many Italian Americans, though I have read that Latinos also use the term. Old-timers, like Grandma, who knew about as many English words as she had fingers and toes, might call it "una saahnweech.")

Snacking went on into the night because my brothers, sister, and I often studied late. This late eating, coupled with substantial regular meals, might lead you to believe that we were a family of hippos. Luckily, we all played sports, which enabled us to ward off obesity. Ironically, I had trouble gaining weight, and Russ looked downright thin in his just-under-six-foot-four frame.

After dinner and a little television, we'd hit the books and the refrigerator. We'd wander around the kitchen or go into the basement and check out the auxiliary fridge. It was not unlike bears foraging for food in the wild. "What's this? Leftover lamb stew? I wonder if we have any meatballs left. Let's see what's under the cake server. Oh, good, chocolate cake. Where did Mom hide the …?" And so it went.

In addition to general snacking, we each had our own quirky favorites. Russ had a thing for shredded wheat and warm milk. He was also extremely fond of pistachios, which in those days were dyed red to hide imperfections in the shells—and make them stand out in the stores. Because he ate them often, from five-cent bags sold at the delicatessen down the block, Russ had perpetually red fingertips.

Maria liked to make ice cream sodas with ginger ale and whatever ice cream was in the house—usually vanilla or Neapolitan (layers of vanilla, strawberry, and chocolate). To this, she added crushed graham crackers. My favorite concoction also included graham crackers. In a tall glass which was once a family-size jar for jelly, I alternated layers of graham crackers and strawberry jam. Then I filled the glass with milk. That combination sounded a lot more appetizing when I was ten than it does now.

In college at the University of Pennsylvania in Philadelphia, snacking was especially important in my fraternity, Delta Tau Delta, which was top-heavy with jocks. Snacking satisfied our primal need for food and was a good excuse to interrupt studying. As with my family, snacking was a serious pursuit. I felt right at home. You could save a little money if you were willing to pick up hoagies and cheesesteaks for other guys, who would pay for yours if you did. "I'll buy if you'll fly" was the slogan for this delivery agreement.

The prime snack foods in Philly were hoagies and cheesesteaks, both local institutions. The tiny shop where I got my cheesesteaks used to have a contraption for melting the cheese that looked like a miniature pants press. Now I think it was an early version of the panini press. Around the corner was Ronnie's, where I'd get my hoagies. I remember the roast beef at Ronnie's, in particular. It was so rare that it mooed.

I still love to snack, but I have to be careful. It is said that what you eat after 6:00 p.m. Is more critical to weight gain than everything you eat before, so I try to relegate my snacking to fruit and perhaps a little cheese. However, there was a three-year period when I was training for three marathons. Running forty to fifty miles a week allowed me to return to those glorious snacking days of yesteryear. "Is there peanut butter in the house? Do we have any of that pork roast left? I thought I saw some of that double-chocolate…"

OLIVE SALAD

Mom used large Greek or Spanish olives for this salad. I did, too, until my wife, Mary, found those olives too acidic. Then I changed to the sweeter, smaller Cerignola and Castelvetrano olives from Italy. One of the keys to this dish is the leafy tops of celery, which give the salad a special flavor. I frequently add some Italian parsley, especially if there aren't many celery leaves. Pepperoncini were not in Mom's original recipe, but she added them because they were always around the house. You may want to omit the pepperoncini until the salad is complete. Then add some or all of it.

1 pound large green olives with pits, such as Cerignola or Castelvetrano

4 ribs celery, including leafy tops

1 medium sweet onion, peeled, halved, and cut into very thin half-moons

3 tablespoons capers, rinsed and drained

1–2 tablespoons Italian parsley (optional)

6 tablespoons olive oil

5 tablespoons cider or wine vinegar

1/2 teaspoon salt

Pepper to taste

1 teaspoon oregano

1/3 cup bottled, sliced pepperoncini, drained (optional)

1. Rinse olives, and pat dry. With the side of a chef's knife or the bottom of a bottle or mallet, crack each olive just enough so the pit is exposed. Put the olives in a mixing bowl.

2. Coarsely chop the leafy parts of the celery, and cut the rest into 1/2-inch-wide crescents. Add the celery and onions to the olives. Add the capers and, if desired, the parsley.

3. Put the olive oil, vinegar, and seasonings in a small jar with a screw-cap top. Shake well, and add to the olive mixture. Add some or all of the pepperoncini, if desired. Mix well, and let marinate in the refrigerator for several hours or up to 24 hours. Let the salad come to room temperature (30 minutes or so) before serving.

CAPONATA

Caponata is a traditional Sicilian dish, the Italian version of the French Provencal favorite ratatouille, though I like to call ratatouille the French version of caponata. One of my favorite snacks as a kid was something called eggplant appetizer, which was made by Progresso and came in little blue cans. It was really caponata, but the term *eggplant appetizer* was more prominent on the label. I'd eat the caponata right out of the can, like World War II C-rations. I wonder if that's how the Italian army ate it.

Though we ate caponata often, Mom didn't start making her own until she was in her sixties or seventies, which was odd, since Grandma brought the recipe with her from Sicily and made it regularly when Mom was growing up. I asked Mom why it took her so long to make it herself.

"Truthfully speaking, I never liked eggplant," she said. "Or should I say, I liked it, but it doesn't like me." That was one of Mom's favorite expressions, a way of saying that eggplant, or perhaps the way it was prepared, did unkind things to her digestive system. She never said, "It gives me gas." Dad would also use euphemisms for gastric distress, such as, "It repeats on me."

I had a cast-iron stomach when I was growing up, so I never fully appreciated what Mom and Dad were saying until I got older and realized I couldn't eat the way I used to.

Despite Mom's issues with eggplant consumption, she still canned a few dozen jars of caponata a year for the rest of us (as well as pickled eggplant). Since caponata is best eaten cold (like revenge, another favorite Sicilian dish) or at room temperature, it's an ideal candidate for canning.

As it said on the side of the Progresso can before the company discontinued making it, caponata makes an ideal hors d'oeuvre or antipasto. At Vincenzo's, my first restaurant in Philadelphia, we served caponata as an appetizer, topped with olive oil–packed tuna fish, strips of roasted red peppers, and toasted pine nuts.

3 large eggplants, about 4 pounds (unpeeled), cut into 1-inch cubes

1 cup olive oil or more, as needed

2 cups celery, cut into 3/8-inch crescents

3 large green bell peppers, cut into 1/2-inch squares (about 4 cups)

3 large onions, chopped medium fine (about 5 cups)

6 cloves garlic, chopped

1 (28-ounce) can Italian plum tomatoes (drained, juice reserved), seeded and chopped

1 (28-ounce) can crushed tomatoes (save the can)

2 tablespoons tomato paste

1/2 cup red wine vinegar

2 cups salad olives or small green pimento-stuffed olives, coarsely chopped

1/2 cup chopped fresh basil

1/2 cup chopped fresh parsley

2 tablespoons granulated sugar

Salt and pepper to taste

5 sterilized, hot canning jars (see Can Do chapter)

1. In a large mixing bowl, liberally sprinkle the eggplant with salt and toss well. Lay out the cubes on sheet pans lined with paper towels for 1/2 hour or more. Squeeze the eggplant gently with the paper towels (and additional paper towels, as needed) to remove the moisture.

2. Put a large heavy-bottom skillet over high heat. Add half the oil. When the oil is very hot but not smoking, add enough eggplant cubes to loosely cover the bottom of the pan. Don't crowd the pan, or the eggplant will steam. Stir the eggplant until it softens and becomes lightly browned. You'll probably need to do this step in at least two, probably three, batches, depending on the size of your skillet.

3. With a slotted spoon, remove the eggplant to a Dutch oven or heavy-bottom pot large enough to hold all the ingredients. Repeat, adding more oil as needed, until all the eggplant is fried.

4. Lower the heat in the skillet to medium, adding a little more oil, if needed. Add the celery, and sauté about 5 minutes without browning. Add to the pot with the eggplant. Repeat with the peppers and onion, adding the garlic when the onions are about half-finished. Be careful not to let the garlic burn.

5. Add the plum and crushed tomatoes to the pot. In the reserved crushed tomato can, mix the tomato paste with the vinegar and reserved juice from the chopped tomatoes. Add to the pot along with the remaining ingredients. Cover, and bring to a simmer. Simmer for 30 minutes, stirring gently every 5 minutes or so. Uncover, and cook 10 minutes more or until sauce is thickened. Vegetables should still be reasonably firm. Taste for seasoning. It should have a subtle sweet-and-sour flavor.

6. Pack in the hot, sterilized canning jars. Seal, and let cool at room temperature for 48 hours.

OLD-FASHIONED NUTRITION

Here's an exchange between Maude and her husband from the 1970s television situation comedy *Maude* that illustrates how views on nutrition have changed over the decades:

Maude: "Here's your breakfast, dear."

Husband: "Oatmeal? Why can't I have bacon and eggs for breakfast?"

Maude: "Too much fat. It'll kill you."

Husband: "My grandfather ate bacon and eggs every day for breakfast, and he lived to be 90."

Maude: "That was before we knew about cholesterol."

It's likely this conversation about cholesterol was influenced by Nathan Pritikin, whose eponymous low-fat diet became world famous. Pritikin died of leukemia at age of 69, though his autopsy showed his arteries were "amazingly unclogged." Famous nutritionist Adelle Davis, who was highly critical of the American diet, died in 1974 of cancer at age 70.

My mother died at age 99, just a few months shy of the century mark. Concepts like cholesterol came late in her life, long after my siblings and I flew the coop. I'm pretty sure she never heard of Adelle Davis. She may have come across the name of Nathan Pritikin but only in passing, like Andrei Gromyko or Giorgio Armani. I don't know how clogged or unclogged her arteries were when she died. All I know is that Mom, like her mother before her, was made the way they don't make 'em anymore. Grandma died at age 83 while still going full tilt. And though Dad died at 62 (primarily from injuries suffered in a car accident), three of his siblings lived to 95 or older, one to 100.

Mom ran rings around most other women her age. While many of them were ready for the rocking chair and the blanket over the knees, Mom was busy cooking, cleaning, sewing, and volunteering at the hospital—for 35 years—where my sister, brothers, and I were born. On Mom's worst day, she could have arm wrestled Adelle Davis out of commission.

I'm all for good nutrition. I work out with a trainer three times a week, walk frequently, and work in the significant yard and garden that wrap around three-fourths of our house. I eat a minimum of junk food. And, yes, like Mom did, I do watch my cholesterol now that we know it's here.

Mom was also a stickler for balanced meals. You had your protein (usually your meat, unless it was your meatless Friday), your starch, your green vegetable, and your salad. So there was no need to eat bran for our fiber, nor did we sprinkle wheat germ over our cereal or swallow our zinc pills with freshly squeezed carrot juice. The closest we got to eating "health food," which is what some people call this stuff, was taking cod liver oil. Cod liver oil wasn't food; it was medicine, like sulfa pills or Vicks VapoRub.

I eat a wide-ranging diet that can be Indian food one day, Italian the next, and Japanese after that. But there are limits. Take tofu. (Please!) Tofu—Calvin Trillin called it "toe food"—is pure vegetable protein. It has very little fat and no cholesterol. And no taste. No matter how you slice it, dice it, steam it, or stir-fry it, it's boring. I could see eating tofu if maybe you're starving, broke, and forced at gunpoint.

Today, there are faux foods made with tofu and other vegan niceties (such as seitan), like faux sausage and faux cheese. I say faux-get it.

My idea of health food is food that tastes good and makes you feel good—like tripe. Mom always had a container or two of tripe in the freezer whenever my siblings or I visited. Tripe remains an obscure cut of meat for most people, along with sweetbreads, hearts, and brains. Many people are turned off by eating animal's organs, though the lining of a cow's stomach, which is what tripe is, doesn't actually fit that description. As a youngster, my brother Russ had a problem with tripe because of the smell during the parboiling process. Russ would wonder, "Why are we burning tires in the house?" (As an adult, Russ became a fan of Mom's tripe.)

For those taken aback by the mere mention of indelicacies like bovine stomach lining, there is hope. Many years ago, I introduced tripe to my friend Howard Coffin, a WASP through and through. He got hooked. When we'd go shopping at the Italian Market in Philadelphia, he looked forward to a bowl of tripe at Shank's Roast Beef, just a block away.

Shank's, long since gone, was a great little place where Italian "health" food abounded, from sausage and greens to veal cutlets to peppers and eggs. You could eat tripe in a large or small bowl at Shank's. The customary accompaniment of grated cheese was provided in little juice bottles, the caps of which had been punctured full of holes. If you were embarrassed by eating tripe in a public place, or if, like me, you couldn't get enough of it, Shank's provided the ultimate in takeout—tripe to go.

All that said, I have to admit my taste for tripe has waned over the years. This, despite the fact that the recipe below is, if you'll pardon my immodesty, better than Mom's. If you do like tripe—and don't mind opening the windows and turning on the exhaust fan full blast, as you may want to do in step 1—you'll love this dish.

TRIPE

Mom didn't use red wine, but it gives added body and flavor. Any full-bodied dry red wine will do, though a rustic red from southern Italy, like a Montepulciano d'Abruzzo or Primitivo, would be a good choice to use in cooking and to drink with the meal. In case you don't know eight to twelve people who will eat tripe, you can freeze part of it, just like Mom did.

6 pounds honeycomb tripe*

3 tablespoons olive oil

3 ribs celery, cut into 1/4-inch dice

1 large onion, finely chopped

2 cloves garlic, chopped fine

1 (28-ounce) can Italian plum tomatoes, seeded and chopped, with juice

1 (28-ounce) can tomato puree

2 (6-ounce) cans tomato paste

2 teaspoons dried oregano

2 bay leaves

1/8–1/4 teaspoon crushed red pepper flakes

Salt and pepper to taste

1 cup dry red wine (optional)

Grated Romano cheese for serving

1. Put the tripe in a large kettle, cover with water, and bring to a boil. Drain, refill with water, and when water boils again, reduce to a simmer for 2 hours. Turn on the exhaust fans full blast and open the windows if you can't tolerate the smell.

2. While the tripe is cooking, put a large Dutch oven (large enough to hold the sauce and tripe) over moderate heat. When hot, add the oil. Add the celery and cook a few minutes. Add onion and cook a few minutes more. Add garlic and cook another minute or two, stirring to prevent garlic from burning.

3. Add the remaining ingredients, except the cheese. Rinse out the tomato paste cans and puree can with 2 puree cans of water and add to the other ingredients. Mix well, and simmer for 45 minutes.

4. Heat the oven to 350 degrees.

5. When the tripe is cooked, drain and rinse with cool water in a large colander. Cut the tripe into strips about 1 1/2 by 1/4 inch. Add to the sauce, and bring to a simmer. Put in the oven, and cook 60–90 minutes or until tripe is tender and just slightly chewy. Serve with grated cheese and crusty Italian bread. Serves 8–12

*Honeycomb tripe comes from a certain part of the cow's stomach and is the most tender and mildest part. It gets its name from the honeycomb pattern on one side.

PASTA E FAGIOLI

Mom's version of macaroni and beans, which is what *pasta e fagioli* means (and what we called it; that Americanization again), was rather bland. So, I—you'll pardon the expression—souped it up. My version is from my *Low-Fat Cooking to Beat the Clock* book. One of the significant changes is using ricotta salata, a tangy sheep's milk cheese from Italy (mainly Sicily) that bears little resemblance to the softer, blander fresh ricotta Mom used. If you can't find ricotta salata, you could use a good-quality feta made with sheep's milk, not the ubiquitous American-style feta made with cow's milk.

My father's side of the family used dried beans that took hours to cook, which Mom didn't (and which I don't think is necessary). Dad's family also added tomatoes.

2 tablespoons olive oil

1 medium to large onion (8–12 ounces), chopped

4 cloves garlic, chopped

1 (7-ounce) jar roasted red bell peppers, drained and chopped

1/2 cup dry white wine

1 1/2 cups vegetable stock

2 (15-ounce) cans cannellini beans, drained and rinsed

2 teaspoons salt, plus additional to taste for seasoning

12 ounces short pasta, such as ziti, rigatoni, penne, or orecchiette

1/2 cup packed fresh basil leaves (or flat-leaf Italian parsley; don't use dried basil)

1/4 teaspoon pepper (or more to taste)

2 ounces ricotta salata

4 teaspoons high-quality extra-virgin olive oil

1. For the pasta, put a 4-quart pot three-quarters full with water over high heat until it reaches a boil.

2. Meanwhile, put a large sauté pan or Dutch oven over medium heat. Add the olive oil. Add the onion, and sauté a few minutes until it begins to soften. Add the garlic, stir, and cook a few minutes more. Add the roasted peppers, stir, and cook a few minutes more. Add the wine and vegetable stock, and bring to a simmer.

3. Add the beans to the sauté pan. Cover, and bring to a boil; then uncover and reduce the heat to a simmer.

4. As soon as the pasta water boils, add 2 teaspoons of salt and the pasta. Stir well, cover, and return to a boil. Stir well again, and cook at a rolling boil until the pasta is done according to package instructions or to your taste.

5. While the pasta cooks, stack the basil leaves, roll into a cigar shape, and cut crosswise into thin ribbons. (Or chop the Italian parsley.) Add the basil (or parsley), 1/4 teaspoon pepper, and salt to taste to the beans. Mash half of the beans with a potato masher or the back of a large spoon to thicken the sauce.

6. Crumble, coarsely chop, or grate the cheese on the large holes of a 4-sided grater. Drain the pasta, reserving a cup of the cooking liquid. Add the pasta to the bean sauce. Combine well, adding some or all of the pasta cooking water if you want it a bit thinner. Adjust for salt and pepper, if needed. Divide the soup equally among 4 soup plates. Sprinkle with the cheese, and drizzle 1 teaspoon of the extra-virgin olive oil over each. Serves 4.

IN LOVE WITH LAMB

There are two kinds of people in this world: those who like lamb and those who don't. The people who don't may be vegetarians or their only exposure to lamb was in school cafeterias, which was enough to make anyone become a vegetarian. I haven't been in a school cafeteria for decades, but in my day in those facilities, the lamb looked more like aluminum siding than meat. It's because they used the standard institutional recipe for roast lamb:

Step 1: Place lamb in 400 degree oven. Cook several hours until meat becomes gray, dry, and thoroughly tasteless. Do not season.

Step 2: Slice meat, and keep on steam table all day.

Step 3: Serve with ugly green mint jelly to kill taste.

Anyone who tried lamb prepared in this fashion could not possibly like it, and anyone who liked lamb wouldn't even recognize it. In such places, I think the government should require warning signs, as they do for cigarettes: "Warning: the Department of Agriculture has determined that this food, in its current state, does not resemble anything that can remotely be considered lamb. The consumption of this food may cause permanent damage to your palate."

The people who like lamb can be subdivided into two groups. There are those who only eat it in restaurants, where they serve leg of lamb, lamb chops, or rack of lamb for two (a practice I've never liked; I'll eat the whole rack myself, please). There's nothing wrong with that. In fact, my wife, Mary, has become somewhat of a connoisseur of rack of lamb. This is a quantum culinary leap for her. She told me she remembers seeing the kind of lamb I described above in college cafeterias, though she can't remember eating it. Mary also came from a family where baked ham was considered exotic. Incidentally, the lamb prepared at La Caravelle, the legendary French restaurant in New York that closed in 2004, still tops Mary's list as the best she's ever tasted.

I'm from the second category of lamb lovers. I'll eat lamb almost any time, whether it's an Indian, Indonesian, or Italian preparation. There are many who may not associate Italians with lamb. There are even Italians who scrunch up their noses and say, "I don't like lamb."

But when I was growing up, we ate lamb often. The closest we got to rack of lamb, however, was shoulder lamb chops. I use the word "*closest*" advisedly here, as in, "The closest car we have to a Rolls-Royce is a Chevy Malibu."

We ate shoulder lamb chops because Mom couldn't afford to feed us the more expensive loin or rib chops. Her children didn't even know they existed, so how could we feel deprived?

This did not mean Mom skimped on quality. On the contrary, she was a fanatic about it. I don't remember shopping with her for lamb chops, but I do remember being with her when she shopped for steak. It was in Sattler's basement in Buffalo. Sattler's was one of those places where you could buy anything, from garden hoses to hot dogs. It was always crowded, but Mom handled herself with the assurance of Moses Malone going for an offensive rebound.

Lest you think that shopping for steak is incongruous with shoulder lamb chops, please remember this was the dawn of history when sirloin steak was 88 cents a pound. Periodically, it went on sale for 68 cents a pound. That's when Mom really went into action.

She'd prowl around the meat department, waiting for the butcher to come out with a fresh platter of steaks. Then, with the speed of a lion pouncing on a wildebeest, she'd grab the poor guy before he had a chance to put the steaks in the meat case, and she'd say, "I'll take this one, that one, and those two."

Shoulder lamb chops were good, if a bit chewy. (Or in the words of my sister, Maria, "They were never really tender.") Mom marinated them in oil, garlic, and lemon juice, though such marinades—in fact, most marinades—don't tenderize tough cuts of meat. Flavor, yes. Tenderize, no. Then she broiled them. If she didn't have time to marinate the lamb, she'd just squeeze some lemon on the chops when they finished cooking.

Today, if I'm going to have lamb chops, I'll splurge and buy a rack or loin chops. Mostly, though, I prefer the cheaper cuts of lamb, as well as beef, veal, and pork, for that matter. About the cheapest cut you can get is a neck of lamb. Mom used the neck to make lamb stew. Lamb stew always seemed like a strange dish for an Italian family, especially since it contained cabbage, not a vegetable Italians often consume. The origin of this dish is not clear. Mom said her mother made it often because it was inexpensive. My guess is that Grandma created it or modified an existing recipe once she arrived here from Sicily in the early part of the twentieth century.

Perhaps that is why it has something I've never seen in any other lamb stew, Italian or not—a ham bone. Grandma probably had a ham bone lying around when she was going to make lamb stew, and she figured, "why not?" Why not, indeed, since Buffalo's most famous dish, Buffalo chicken wings, was created on the fly by combining three incongruous ingredients—deep-fried chicken wings in hot sauce, blue cheese dressing, and celery sticks.

For this recipe, you can use the neck or the breast of lamb or even shoulder lamb chops. Mom preferred the neck because it's less fibrous. Both cuts are extremely flavorful and great bargains. As with all cheaper pieces of meat, long, slow cooking with liquid is required, but the result is worth waiting for.

We all loved Mom's lamb stew, except Russ, the picky eater of the family. "First, you had to go through all that crap (i.e., vegetables) to get to the meat—I especially hated the cabbage," he said. "Then when you got to the meat, there were too many bones. I think it should have been called 'lamb bone stew' instead of lamb stew."

When we were living on our own, my brother Frank and I both made Mom's lamb stew during the winter months. While mine is relatively faithful to Mom's original recipe, Frank changed it somewhat with the addition of things like turnips, mushrooms, and thyme. Maria rarely cooked for herself but placed her order with Mom when she was going to visit. Yes, I do mean *order*. You see, after you called Mom to tell her you were coming for a visit, she immediately began to plan a menu for the entire period you'd be there. I think she had a checklist by the phone, ready for our calls. Shortly after the usual pleasantries, she'd say, "Now what would you like me to make for you?" Then she'd rattle off the choices. "Do you want lasagna, braciola, artichokes …" This is somewhat misleading, however, because Mom had prepared most of these dishes ahead of time and stuck them in the freezer. So it was really, "What would you like me to defrost?"

As good as Mom's lamb stew is, you need not relegate the neck and breast to that recipe alone. The neck can be used in any stew dish. The breast is more versatile. It can be boned and stuffed with a variety of fillings, from spinach and ricotta to seasoned bread crumbs and sausage, to rice, pine nuts, and currants. You can also eat it as you would pork or beef ribs. Unlike those two varieties, some additional preparation is required, but the finished product is equally satisfying.

MOM'S SICILIAN LAMB STEW

This is a good recipe to make after you've had a ham for a holiday dinner instead of using the ham bone for split-pea or bean soup. You could also use a smoked pork hock. Or, if you frequent a deli that sells prosciutto, ask them for an end piece, which can't be used for slicing. This is also one of the many dishes in which Mom used her canned tomatoes.

My niece Katie tested this recipe and provided some very valuable feedback, though she admits to not being a particularly skillful cook. As with many less-experienced cooks, she asked a lot of basic questions, like, "What kind of potatoes?" The answer is just about any kind, except sweet potatoes or baking potatoes. If you're using small red-skinned or yellow potatoes, you don't have to peel them. Just give them a good scrubbing.

We never minded dealing with the lamb bones—except Russ. But if your family has a picky eater, use boneless lamb stew meat for this recipe. Figure about 2.5 pounds.

5–6 pounds breast of lamb or lamb necks or combination of the two

Salt and pepper to taste

1 (2-pound) head of green cabbage, cut in wedges about 1 inch wide

1 pound carrots, cut in 1-inch pieces, larger if the carrots are thin

2 medium onions, thickly sliced

About 3 pounds potatoes, peeled (or not), and cut into 1 to 1 1/2–inch chunks

1 quart of Mom's Canned Tomatoes (see Can Do chapter), chopped, or 1 (28-ounce) can diced tomatoes, either with their juices

2 bay leaves

1/2 teaspoon red pepper flakes, or to taste

2 teaspoons oregano

1 good-sized ham bone or 2 smoked hocks

2 cups chicken or beef broth or water

1. Heat an oven to 500 degrees.

2. If using breast of lamb, cut into ribs similar in size to spareribs. Season the lamb with salt and pepper, and place on a rack over a roasting or broiler pan. Bake until well browned on all sides. (This will considerably reduce the greasiness of the dish.) Remove the lamb from the oven, and reduce the oven temperature to 350 degrees.

3. Layer the ingredients in a large heavy casserole dish or Dutch oven as follows: Half each of the meat, cabbage, carrots, potatoes, tomatoes and their juice, onions, and seasonings. Place ham bone in the center and add the remaining ingredients in the same order. Pour the broth over.

4. Cover, and bake in the oven for about 2 hours or until lamb is fork-tender. Stir a few times during the cooking.

5. Serve with plenty of crusty Italian bread and a green salad. A fruity Lambrusco or rustic Montepulciano d'Abruzzo would go nicely. Serves 4–6.

SHOULDER LAMB CHOPS

Because shoulder lamb chops were the only kind of lamb chops I knew, I was surprised to find loin and rib lamb chops for the first time when I lived off campus my senior year in college. I wondered why Mom never served them to us. When I saw the prices, I realized why.

Shoulder lamb chops are chewier than their more expensive loin and rib cousins. To mitigate this chewiness, they should be cooked quickly under intense heat, leaving the interior medium rare to medium. For people who can't tolerate red meat with pink or red interiors—or the tougher nature of grilled shoulder chops—they can be braised, as in the recipe below for Smothered Lamb Chops. The lamb in the recipe below can also be cooked in a grill pan on top of the stove, grilled over a charcoal fire, or in the way I've described in the method below. Serve with Fried Potatoes with Peppers and Onions, the recipe for which is in this chapter.

1/2 cup olive oil

Juice from one lemon

2 cloves garlic, peeled and put through a press

Salt and pepper to taste

4 shoulder lamb chops, about 8 ounces each

1. To make the marinade, combine all ingredients, except lamb, in a dish large enough to hold the lamb chops without overlapping.

2. Put the lamb chops in the marinade, and coat well on both sides. Refrigerate for 2 hours, turning once or twice. Remove to room temperature 30 minutes before cooking, and turn the chops over to coat well again.

3. Turn on the broiler. Put a cast-iron skillet or a grill pan large enough to hold the lamb chops in one layer on a rack under the broiler, about four inches from the heat source, for 15 minutes. Remove chops from marinade. Take the skillet from the broiler, and add the chops. Put the skillet under the broiler for 2 minutes on each side for medium rare but no more than 2 1/2 minutes on each side for medium. Remove the chops to a platter, and cover loosely with foil for 5 minutes. Serves 4.

SMOTHERED LAMB CHOPS WITH ORZO

This recipe is from my first *Cooking to Beat the Clock* book (Chronicle), which was named one of the ten best cookbooks of the year by Amazon.com. Instead of orzo, you could use couscous or rice.

1 cup orzo

2 3/4 cups chicken stock, divided

4 shoulder lamb chops, about 8 ounces each

Salt and pepper to taste

1 tablespoon olive oil

1 medium onion, about 8 ounces

2 cloves garlic

1 anchovy fillet

24 small pimiento-stuffed olives, coarsely chopped, or salad olives

2 teaspoons fresh rosemary, chopped, or 1 teaspoon dried, crushed

1 tablespoon small capers, drained

1. Put the orzo in a microwavable container with a cover. Add 2 1/4 cups of the chicken stock. Cover and cook on high power for 11 minutes. (Lower the power if the orzo looks like it might overflow.) Keep covered until ready to serve. (You can also cook the orzo on the stove. It will take about the same time as the microwave.)

2. While the orzo cooks, put over high heat a skillet large enough to hold all the lamb chops in one layer. Season the chops with salt and pepper. Put the olive oil in the skillet and swirl to distribute. Add the chops and brown on each side for 2 minutes.

3. While the lamb cooks, peel, halve, and thinly slice the onion. When the lamb chops have browned, remove them to a platter and loosely cover with foil. Lower the heat under the skillet to medium, and add the onion. Cook a few minutes while you peel the garlic and chop it with the anchovy fillet. Add them to the onion. Lower the heat if the onion or garlic start to get too brown.

4. Add the olives, rosemary, and capers to the skillet, and sauté the mixture for 2 minutes. Add the remaining 1/2 cup chicken stock, and mix well, scraping any bits from the bottom of the pan. Bring to a simmer.

5. Add the lamb chops to the skillet, along with any liquid accumulated from the platter. Spoon an equal amount of the vegetable mixture on top of each chop. Cover and simmer for 15–20 minutes, adding a bit more stock (or water) if too dry. To serve, put an equal amount of orzo on individual plates, add a lamb chop, and spoon the sauce over it. Serves 4.

ROASTED PEPPERS

Though roasted peppers have become increasingly popular in recent years—I always keep a jar or two of them in my pantry—I've eaten freshly roasted peppers as far back as I can remember. Generally, we had them with meats like steak and shoulder lamb chops. Mom prepared the peppers very simply with an olive oil blend, salt, and pepper. I prefer more flavorful extra-virgin olive oil, a little vinegar, and a "touch" of garlic.

(When I was food editor of the *San Jose Mercury News*, I was asked to emcee the annual cook-off at the Gilroy Garlic Festival, cofounded by Don Christopher, the largest garlic producer in the country. Don, who died in 2022, told me something about garlic I'll never forget. He said the more you do to garlic, the more flavor you get out of it. For the most flavor, finely chop it, or put it through a garlic press. For that "touch" of garlic in this or any other dish, crush the clove with the side of the knife and peel. Then put the whole crushed clove, still intact, in a sauce or marinade. Or in salad dressing, which is what Mom did. Discard the garlic when serving or when you've got the amount of garlic flavor you want.)

Mom used green bell peppers because they were cheaper than the red ones. The latter, which I prefer, are left on the vine longer, which gives them a sweeter taste and more vitamins A and C. Red bell peppers are also more digestible (i.e., they are less likely to "repeat" on you).

4 large green or red bell peppers

1/2 cup olive oil

2–3 tablespoons balsamic or very good red wine vinegar

1 clove garlic

Salt and pepper to taste

1. Roast the peppers under a broiler or on a charcoal grill until they blister and blacken. Turn them periodically to cook them evenly all around. Put the peppers in a sealed plastic bag or a covered bowl until they are cool enough to handle.

2. Meanwhile, mix the oil and vinegar in a shallow dish or pan large enough to hold the peppers in one layer. With the side of a chef's knife, press firmly on, or lightly pound, the garlic and peel it. (It should still be intact.) Add it to the oil and vinegar. Season with salt and pepper, and mix well.

3. Peel the skins off the peppers, and remove the stems and seeds. You can scrape off some of the difficult skin parts with a butter knife, but if some blackened skin remains, it's fine. Do not rinse under water, which will dilute the flavor. Cut into 1/2-inch-wide strips.

4. Combine the peppers and marinade thoroughly, and let sit 1 hour or longer. If more than 2 hours, refrigerate but bring to room temperature before serving. Discard garlic before serving. Serves 4.

FRIED POTATOES WITH PEPPERS AND ONIONS

This is another dish we often had with lamb chops. Mom usually cooked it (and many other dishes) with bacon fat. Any time she cooked bacon, she drained the fat and stored it in the refrigerator. The bacon fat gives this dish a special flavor.

3 tablespoons bacon fat

4 medium-large potatoes, peeled and sliced 1/8 inch thick

1 small green pepper, cut into 1/4-inch strips

1 medium onion, cut into 1/4-inch slices

Salt and pepper to taste

1 teaspoon paprika

3 cloves garlic, chopped

1. Put a large cast-iron or other heavy-bottom skillet over medium heat. Add the bacon fat. When the bacon fat is hot, add the potatoes, peppers, onions, salt, pepper, and paprika. Mix well. Cover, and cook over low heat for 10–15 minutes. Turn over once or twice with a wide spatula.

2. Remove the cover, add the garlic, and raise the heat slightly. Stir periodically until the potatoes are lightly browned and just tender, 5–10 minutes. Serves 4.

CAN II

Mom would arrive late to the farmers' market, just as the farmers were packing up to go home. After scanning the assemblage, she'd pick out the farmer with the best produce and announce, "Give me a good price, and I'll take the whole lot." The farmer, preferring to sell rather than schlep leftover produce back to the farm, almost always agreed.

The "whole lot," incidentally, was not measured in pounds, but in bushels. Mom remembered her all-time canning high of 25 bushels of tomatoes. That translated into about 400 quarts!

My brothers, sister, and I all have fond memories of the canning season. Those favorable remembrances may be partly because we were never enlisted to do any of the heavy work. We'd pop in and out of the basement to take a break from street football or backyard basketball. Mom, Aunt Sandy, and Grandma were there, hour after hour, scarves around their heads, their aprons stained with tomatoes, peaches, and pears, as they peeled and squeezed and stuffed jar after jar of produce at its very peak.

My brother Frank refers to the "canning factory in the basement"—which it was—with vivid smells of peaches and pears. "Peaches were my favorite," said Frank. "I guess it's genetic because my son Paul loves them too." My sister, Maria, was partial to pears, though she liked to "squish the tomatoes." Russ wondered aloud, "How many peaches has Mom's paring knife peeled? That knife deserves to be in the Smithsonian."

When we lived in the old neighborhood, upstairs from Grandma, there was a grape arbor in the backyard. The grapes were the blue-purple Concord and green Niagara varieties so prevalent in Upstate New York. The Concord grapes were great for jam but not so much for wine, unless you were making sickeningly sweet kosher wines.

Salvatore Giglia, my maternal grandfather, used to make wine using a big wine press in the basement, not with Concord or Niagara grapes but with purchased zinfandel grapes from California. (Italian Americans have always had an affinity for zinfandel, which early Italian immigrants frequently planted in California and which was once thought to be—and later found out not to be—the same as the Italian Primitivo grape.) But the winery at 457 Fargo Avenue ended when Grandpa died a few years before I was born. So that wine press sat idle next to the coal bin, both relics of another era.

(As the second-born son, I was supposed to be named after my mother's father, which was the custom in Italian families. The firstborn son was named after the paternal grandfather, Francesco. But just as my uncles Colangelo and Balthazar became Charlie and Albert, my older brother became Frank instead of Francesco, and I became Sam instead of Salvatore. My given name is Samuel, which I always wished could have just been Sam because that's what everyone has called me, except for teachers, nuns, and the IRS.)

Though they weren't used for wine, the grapes from the backyard still served a useful purpose. In addition to being ammunition for grape fights, they were great for eating out of hand as a snack. There was no need to wash them because you didn't eat the thick skin anyway. Instead, you squeezed one end of the grape and the center popped into your mouth. My wife, Mary, who is from Corning, New York, still loves to do this.

One of the first things my father did after signing the settlement papers on the new house on Lovering Avenue in North Buffalo was to build a grape arbor in the backyard. To our neighbors in the then-predominately Jewish section of Buffalo, this may have seemed like the proverbial "There goes the neighborhood." But soon, they accepted us, our grapes, and the other Italians who followed us.

It took about three years for the arbor to bear fruit. When our first crop of grapes was picked, Mom was ready to make her grape jelly. Mom turned out grape jelly so good it made you forget the existence of Welch's.

Dad had a ritual every time he opened a jar of grape jelly. After he removed the paraffin that sealed the top of the jar, he'd skim the top layer of jelly and throw it out. Whenever we asked him why he did this, he gave us a stern look, which telegraphed a message somewhere between "I can't help it; that's the way I am," and "Shut up; I don't have to give you a reason. I'm your father."

In recent years, we have found out that Dad was on to something when he removed every iota of wax from the jam jar. Apparently, paraffin does not create a sufficient seal to prevent mold from forming. And according to the National Center for Home Food Preservation, that mold wasn't as harmless as it was once thought. That said, no one in our house got sick from spoiled jelly.

The NCHFP might also have blanched at what Mom used to strain the grape juice before it was put into jars. Old pillowcases. Mom threatened me with bodily harm if I told anyone about the pillowcases. So, please, keep it under your hat.

CANNED PEACHES

This recipe makes three quarts, assuming that the peaches are free of blemishes. However, it's safe to assume that at least a few peaches might not be pristine, so buy a few extra peaches to compensate.

6 pounds or more of ripe, quality freestone peaches

2 cups sugar

3 cups water

3 sterilized quart jars with lids (see Can Do chapter for sterilizing instructions)

1. Bring a medium- to large-sized pot to a boil and reduce to a simmer. Meanwhile, fill a small tub with cold water. In batches, blanch the peaches for a minute in the simmering water. Then put them in the cold water. When the peaches are cool enough to handle, cut them in half along the "seams." Remove the pits and set aside three of them. Peel the peach halves, remove any blemishes, and put them in cold water.

2. In a medium-size bowl or other container, combine the sugar and water just until the sugar dissolves. (No need to heat the mixture to form a syrup.)

3. Put a peach pit at the bottom of each jar, and add peach halves, hollow side down, until each jar is filled to within 1/2 inch of the top. Add the sugar water to within 1/2 inch of the top. Seal snugly but not tightly by hand.

4. Put the jars in a wire rack that fits inside a kettle. Fill the kettle with tepid water to cover the jars. Bring to a boil. Boil gently for 15 minutes.

5. Remove the jars from the kettle, seal tightly, and let cool for 48 hours. Makes 3 quarts.

GUGINO BELLINI

The Bellini, created at Harry's Bar in Venice in the summer of 1948—the year I was born!—was originally made with white peach puree and prosecco, the sparkling wine of Northeast Italy. My wife, Mary, and I served Bellinis at our wedding reception. But we used Spanish cava instead of prosecco because the former has more body to stand up to the peach puree, which was orange-yellow instead of white.

1/2 cup chopped canned peaches, preferably homemade

1/2 cup syrup from canned peaches

1 bottle sparkling wine

4 teaspoons grenadine (optional)

1. Combine the peaches and syrup in a blender or food processor until thoroughly mixed. (I prefer a food processor, which makes the result less homogenized.)

2. Pour 2 tablespoons of the peach mixture into each of four chilled champagne flutes. Gently fill with the sparkling wine to an inch or so from the top. Give each glass a gentle stir. If desired, drop a teaspoon of grenadine down the center of each glass before serving. Serves 4.

MORE ON AUNT SANDY'S COOKIES

Since I first wrote about Aunt Sandy and her fabulous cookies in the *Philadelphia Daily News* in 1983 (which was the basis for the "Have a Cookie" chapter in this book), I had wanted to do another story on her, if for no other reason than to share more of her cookie recipes. That second story never materialized, but less than two years later, I had the opportunity to directly benefit from Aunt Sandy's cookies in the same way so many of her nieces, nephews, cousins, and friends have for decades. I got married.

Just as she had done numerous times before, Aunt Sandy made up a huge batch of her cookies for the occasion. And just as I remembered from weddings thirty years before in banquet halls in Buffalo, NY, all the guests' tables were supplied with large plates of cookies. They went as well with stir-fried duck in 1985 as they did with chicken cacciatore in 1955.

Aunt Sandy and my mother started making cookies when they were teenagers. They had to learn themselves because Grandma was not a cookie-maker. They initially baked for family St. Joseph's tables. Aunt Sandy's first public display was at the wedding of her girlfriend, who got married at the ripe age of seventeen.

Aunt Sandy, who never married, lived with Grandma on the first floor of a two-story house at 457 Fargo Avenue on Buffalo's West Side. We lived on the second floor until 1957, when Mom and Dad bought a house at 169 Lovering Avenue in North Buffalo.

Grandma died in the winter of 1967, eight or nine months after my father died. Then Aunt Sandy moved upstairs from Mom, an interesting reversal of my early youth. I remember going up and down the stairs a lot on Fargo Avenue, usually the back stairs. But what I remember most was the front stairs; more specifically, what was contained underneath those stairs. Cookies!

The room underneath the stairs was one of those peculiar rooms you find in older houses—too large to be a closet and too small to be a bedroom. It became a catchall room for things like a sewing machine, boxes, clothes, and anything else for which a place couldn't be found. It was always cool and thus was a perfect repository for the endless amount of cookies on hand.

Well into our adulthood, my brother Russ divulged one of his childhood secrets about that room and Aunt Sandy's cookies. When no one was looking, he would sneak into the room and devour cookies. But to cover his tracks, he'd eat an entire boxful. That way, he figured, no one would notice. If he had eaten half a box, his logic went, it would be obvious that someone was filching cookies. Of course, it was important to destroy the box as well. Russ's favorite cookies were butterballs. "I could eat a ton of those," he said.

Even after Aunt Sandy was confined to a wheelchair because of paralysis in her legs, it didn't stop her from baking cookies. A few years before she became hospitalized, I went upstairs to talk to her about her favorite subject.

Aunt Sandy's cookie recipes were stuck in an envelope, along with a ring-binder notebook, stashed in the pantry near the cornflakes. One recipe particularly intrigued me. It was something called "Jew bread," which sounds more than mildly anti-Semitic. I finally asked Aunt Sandy how she got the name. She said, "A Jewish lady gave me the recipe."

Another one of her recipes was for Danish puffs. These are cream puffs that may or may not be Danish. "My girlfriend gave me this recipe twenty years ago," Aunt Sandy said. "She gets burned up because her puffs don't come out as good as mine. I told her it's because she spread the dough. Now, she doesn't spread the dough anymore, but her puffs still aren't as good as mine."

Sifting through Aunt Sandy's recipes was like doing research on papyrus scrolls in an Egyptian museum. But the time spent was well worth it because these are treasures that deserve to live on. Below are more of Aunt Sandy's cookie recipes, along with some hints from the master.

Aunt Sandy's Helpful Hints for Better Cookies

- Don't skimp on your shortening. "A little more won't hurt." Aunt Sandy used Crisco.
- Use a wooden spoon to mix your ingredients, unless the recipe specifically states otherwise.
- "Never over-flour your cookie." If you press your finger into the cookie dough and it comes out clean, you've got enough flour. Sometimes when you have too much flour, you can taste it.
- Always sift your flour, even if it's pre-sifted.
- I would also add to check the temperature of your oven with an oven thermometer. Home ovens are notoriously off, sometimes by as much as 25 degrees.

Butterball cookies
(Photo credit: Caroline Eberle)

BUTTERBALLS

1 cup butter at room temperature

1/4 cup granulated sugar

Pinch of salt

3/4 cup finely chopped walnuts

2 3/4 cups cake flour (not self-rising)

Powdered sugar, about 1 cup

1. Heat the oven to 350 degrees.
2. In a mixing bowl, cream the butter with an electric mixer. Add the granulated sugar and salt, and beat well. Add the nuts and flour, and work the dough until all ingredients are thoroughly mixed. Roll the dough into a ball, cover with plastic wrap, and refrigerate 1 1/2 hours or until dough is firm. (Dough can be made several days ahead.)
3. Allow the dough to come to room temperature. Form into balls slightly smaller than unshelled walnuts. If the dough seems too dry or stiff, squeeze it with your hand before forming the balls.
4. Put the balls on a baking sheet—about an inch apart—and bake for 18 minutes. Leave the cookies on the baking sheet, and put the baking sheet on a rack to cool. When cool, roll in powdered sugar. Makes about 40 cookies.

MOCHA NUT CRESCENTS

1 cup softened butter

1/2 cup granulated sugar

2 teaspoons vanilla

2 teaspoons powdered (not granules) instant coffee

1/4 cup cocoa powder

1/2 teaspoon salt

1 3/4 cups all-purpose flour, sifted

2 cups very finely chopped pecans or walnuts

Powdered sugar

1. Heat the oven to 325 degrees.
2. In a mixing bowl, cream the butter with an electric mixer. Add the granulated sugar, and beat until fluffy. Add the vanilla, and continue beating. Add the coffee, cocoa powder, and the salt. Gradually add in the flour. When the flour is fully incorporated, fold in the nuts, combining thoroughly.
3. Form the dough into balls about 1 inch in diameter. Roll each ball out with your hand to a length of about 3 inches. Then curl the ends to form a crescent shape, gently pinching the ends. Put them on cookie sheets—about an inch apart—and bake for 15 minutes. Cool, and sprinkle with powdered sugar. Makes about 4 dozen cookies.

THE IMPRECISE BUT DELICIOUS WORLD OF ANNA GUGINO

Holding her left hand cupped upward, Anna Gugino poured salt into her palm and said, "This is how much salt I use for three pounds of flour. How much would you say that is?" Obviously, Aunt Sandy was not the only one who winged it with recipes.

Mom was making billulata, an old family favorite. It's a kind of stromboli with a meat, cheese, and onion stuffing. (See Without Bread chapter on page 75.) This was my explanation to my friend Howard Coffin, who replied, "Oh great, that doesn't tell me anything. It's like a Serbo-Croatian explaining a dish by saying, 'Oxfek is a kind of Shumat with a meat, cheese, and onion stuffing.'"

Mom's cooking was a lot like Elizabeth David's. David was a cook and chronicler of mostly Mediterranean foods, particularly French. Her recipes were not neatly laid out in great detail like Julia Child's. Rather, they flowed from the text of the book. As a result, recipes had phrases like "some chopped parsley" and "a little olive oil."

I had been collecting and working out Mom's recipes for years. Some worked well; others did not. Since Mom had been making these dishes for as long as I can remember, it was clear I was missing something. When the peach pie recipe didn't quite work out, I called her to find out why.

"Mom, the pie crust for the peach pie was a little doughy."

"Did you roll it out thin?"

"How thin?"

"Thin enough so it won't be doughy."

As we continued to talk, I realized that the written (or spoken) word was insufficient to translate all of Mom's recipes fully. So, with pen, pad, and camera in hand, I trekked north to Buffalo to watch her make the dishes I had eaten for over four decades.

I arrived late on a Friday night and had a snack of meatballs and braciola before I went to bed. The next morning, Mom was ready to make pies. She always made her pies early in the morning or late at night.

"To the flour, you add one heaping tablespoon of shortening," Mom said as she scooped out a mound of Crisco. But her measuring device wasn't a tablespoon or any kind of spoon at all. It was a large serving fork.

"That's a tablespoon?" I asked incredulously. Then I wrote down, "Add large mound of shortening to flour."

"That's a *heaping* tablespoon" said Mom, correcting me.

In the margin, I jotted, "Buy a large serving fork to measure out heaping tablespoons."

It turns out that the serving fork had another purpose in addition to measuring out "tablespoons." After adding water to the shortening and flour, she used the fork to combine them. I had used my hands, which was a mistake.

"The warmth of the hands is no good," Mom declared, as if quoting some ancient Chinese proverb.

Working quickly was important too. Overworking will produce a tough dough. Mom's hands moved with the speed of Ozzie Smith turning a double play. Once the water, flour, and shortening are combined to form a somewhat sticky mass, the cookbooks tell you the dough should rest for an hour or so to let the gluten in the flour do whatever the gluten in the flour is supposed to do. Even if Mom knew what that was, she wasn't about to wait. She was ready to roll out her dough.

Mom had a foolproof method for rolling out dough so that it never stuck to the rolling pin or work surface. First, she put a large cutting board, about 24 inches by 20 inches, on the kitchen table. The round kitchen table was Mom's work area. She didn't have butcher block tables or stainless-steel counters with marble slabs, like the ones you see on television or in homes of the wealthy, where people didn't cook one-tenth the amount of food Mom did. Mom covered the board with a sturdy white cotton canvas cloth that was somewhat larger than a dish towel and somewhat smaller than a tablecloth. Mom had this cloth for years. "I wouldn't give it up for anything," she said with the same kind of certainty and reverence she had for her rosary, which she said twice a day.

She felt just as strongly about the elasticized sleeve that she slid over the rolling pin. The sleeve showed signs of wear over the years, but Mom couldn't find another, so she was constantly mending it. Today, you can buy both the sleeve (referred to as a rolling pin cover) and cloth (called a pastry cloth) from a variety of cookware stores and sources online.

Mom rolled out the dough with ease, then gently laid it inside a pie plate. Again, the dough should be handled as little as possible. ("Don't pull your crust," Mom admonished.) The excess dough was cut with scissors, leaving a half inch overhang all around the edge.

I don't recall ever seeing the final two steps before. The reason may be that Mom did them so quickly that they were over before you could say "lemon meringue." (See Tucking and Pinching the Dough in The Perfect End to a Meal chapter on page 71.)

Prick the bottom and sides of the shell with a fork and bake in a 350 degree oven until it's done.

"When is it done, Mom?"

"When it's lightly browned."

"How long does that take?"

"I don't know. I've never timed it. I just keep looking."

"What happens if it burns?"

"Scrape off any burned edges with a knife while the pie shell is still hot."

When I made the filling for Mom's coconut cream pie, the filling was a bit runny. While watching her make it, I realized my mistake. Mom added three "heaping" tablespoons of cornstarch to the sugar and eggs. Emphasizing what I had already observed with the shortening for the pie crust, Mom said, "When I say 'heaping,' I mean *heaping*!" Then she scooped out what looked like enough cornstarch to stiffen a dozen pie fillings into rigor mortis.

(Despite translating Mom's heaping tablespoons into regular tablespoons, it still took me a few tries to get the amount of cornstarch right. Six normal tablespoons became seven, then half a cup.)

Once you master the heaping tablespoon concept, the next somewhat tricky step is the addition of scalded milk to the eggs. You need to do this slowly to prevent the eggs from curdling. "Mrs. DeGroat showed me this in seventh grade," said Mom. (Milk scalds at 170 degrees, but I lowered the temperature in the recipe as a hedge against the eggs curdling.)

When the cream mixture has thickened, the shredded coconut is added. Mom measured out 3/4 cup of coconut and dumped it in. Then she threw in some more. "I like a lot of coconut," she said, as if she was following a recipe that read, "Throw in more coconut if you really like it." Then Mom took a teaspoon, not a measuring spoon, from the drawer and measured out vanilla to add to the filling.

"Is that your measuring spoon, Mom?"

"No, I don't usually measure out the vanilla, but since you're writing this down, I thought I would this time."

"Don't change your style on my account."

"OK. You want to know how much 3/4 teaspoon of vanilla is? This is 3/4 teaspoon of vanilla."

Mom poured out the vanilla straight from the bottle as I started to laugh, even though her measuring techniques were probably as accurate, or at least as consistent, as any measuring spoons. "Don't get smart with your mother," she scolded, only half seriously. (Sometimes, Mom echoed what Grandma said to her sons: "You no so smart because you go to college." All three of Mom's brothers went to college, but Mom never finished high school.)

Mom added the filling to the baked pie shell and whipped the egg whites for the meringue. I had a problem with "weeping" meringue (i.e., meringue that separated), and Mom explained that it was caused by undissolved sugar in the egg whites. That's why she used powdered sugar.

The meringue was dusted with more coconut and baked in a 300 degree oven until—you guessed it—it was done. "Done" was lightly browned.

The following recipes are for peach pie and apple pie. For other pie recipes, see the chapters The Perfect End to a Meal (coconut cream and lemon meringue) and There's No Place Like Home for the Holidays (pumpkin).

APPLE PIE

Mom used Rhode Island Greening apples, sometimes referred to as just "Greening" apples, which many consider the quintessential apple for American-style apple pie. Though it's still grown in northeastern United States—not surprisingly, it's the state fruit of Rhode Island—I haven't seen it for some time. Granny Smith might be an acceptable alternative. My late mother-in-law, Madge Keane, who made a pretty fair apple pie herself—the recipe for which is in my first book, *Eat Fresh, Stay Healthy* (Macmillan)—used Northern Spy, which is also a Northeastern apple but not widely available. When I wrote about apple pie for my "Tastes" column in *Wine Spectator* magazine, the dessert-makers I interviewed were all over the map with their favorites. My advice? Use any firm, tart apple or, better yet, a combination of apples, such as Stayman, Winesap, or Jonathan.

Crust

2 1/2 cups flour

1 teaspoon salt

3/4 cup plus 2 tablespoons chilled shortening (14 tablespoons in all)

Ice water, about 8 tablespoons

Filling

About 3 pounds of apples (enough to yield 6 cups when cored, peeled, and sliced)

1/2 cup brown sugar

1/4 cup granulated sugar

1/2 teaspoon cinnamon

1/4 teaspoon nutmeg

3 teaspoons lemon juice

2 1/2 tablespoons cornstarch or flour

1/8 teaspoon salt

2 tablespoons butter

1. For the crust, combine the flour and salt in a large mixing bowl. Add the shortening, breaking it up with a large spoon, fork, or pastry cutter until you get a coarse-meal texture. Add just enough ice water to bind. Don't overhandle the dough. It should be just slightly sticky. (You can do the above in a food processor using the pulse bar to prevent overmixing.) Cover the dough in plastic wrap, and refrigerate at least 30 minutes.

2. Peel and core the apples. Cut them in half and cut the halves into slices about 1/8- to 1/4-inch thick. In a medium-large mixing bowl, combine the apples with all the other filling ingredients, except the butter. Mix well, and set aside.

3. Heat the oven to 400 degrees.

4. Roll out 1/2 of the dough, large enough to line a 9- or 10-inch pie plate. Trim the overhanging dough so it extends 1/2 to 3/4 inch over the edge.

5. Pour the filling into the pie shell, mounding it slightly in the center. Dot with the butter.

6. Roll out the remaining dough, and place on top of the pie. It should just fit the top completely without overhanging. Trim as necessary to fit. With well-floured fingers, curl the bottom edge over the top all around the pie to secure. Then make a wave-like edge by pushing the dough from the

outside with your left forefinger into an opening of about one inch between your right forefinger and thumb. Flour your fingertips frequently as you do this around the edges of the pie.

7. Make 2 or 3 slits in the top of the pie to let steam escape. Bake for 50 minutes, or until golden brown. Serves 6–8.

PEACH PIE

The type of peaches doesn't much matter as long as they are freestone, meaning the stone easily comes away from the flesh.

Crust

See ingredients in the Apple Pie recipe.

Filling

5 cups ripe but still somewhat firm peaches, peeled and cut into slices 1/4 to 3/8 inch thick

1/2 cup brown sugar

1/2 cup granulated sugar

3 tablespoons cornstarch

1/4 to 1/2 teaspoon nutmeg

1/2 teaspoon cinnamon

1/8 teaspoon salt

1 tablespoon lemon juice

2 tablespoons butter

1. For the crust, follow directions in the first step of the Apple Pie recipe.

2. Meanwhile, for the filling, combine the peaches with brown sugar and granulated sugar in a bowl. Toss one or two more times over the next 15 to 20 minutes. Drain in a colander over a bowl to catch the juice that will come from the peaches. You should have about 1/2 cup.

3. Whisk the cornstarch into the peach juice until well combined. Add the nutmeg, cinnamon, salt, and lemon juice. Set aside.

4. Heat the oven to 400 degrees. Roll out the dough for the bottom of the pie, as in step 4 of the Apple Pie recipe.

5. Combine the peach slices with the corn starch mixture, and pour into the pie shell. Mound it slightly in the center. Dot with butter.

6. Roll out the dough for the top of the pie as in step 6 of the Apple Pie recipe.

7. Bake in the oven until lightly browned, about 50 minutes. Serve warm or at room temperature. Serves about 6.

PICNICS

My family had a very simple philosophy about picnics. You did everything you would normally do on that day, except you did it outdoors instead of indoors. Since we had pasta almost every Sunday, we saw no reason to change, simply because we'd be eating on a picnic table instead of a kitchen or dining room table.

It never occurred to us that we were crazy, though I can't vouch for the people around us at the picnic grounds. The sauce had been made the day before. To simplify things (somewhat), the pasta was usually lasagna. It was easy to transport and kept its heat, the latter being of questionable value when the outside temperature was 85 degrees.

Whenever we had lasagna (indoors or out), Mom always made a batch of baked macaroni for her older brother Alphonso (Big Al), or, as Dad used to call him, "Al with the phonso" to distinguish him from his younger brother Albert (Little Al), though Dad never called him "Al with the bert."

You see, Uncle Alphonso didn't eat cheese—or at least not consciously so. (Can you imagine an Italian who doesn't eat cheese?) But when I looked at Mom's recipe for baked macaroni—given to her by Grandma—I noticed it had something peculiar.

"Mom, this recipe has cheese in it."

"Yes, I know, dear."

"But didn't you make this for Uncle Al because he doesn't eat cheese?"

"Oh, he ate lots of things with cheese in it. We just didn't tell him."

Mom went on to say that if there was a piece of cheese on top of something, like pizza, Uncle Al wouldn't eat it. But if you hid the cheese inside the dish, he'd eat it. It wasn't as if he was allergic to cheese, like someone with a peanut allergy. He didn't go into formaggio anaphylactic shock or anything. Nor did anyone know why Uncle Al didn't like cheese. (For the record, he didn't like strawberries either, but it was harder to hide strawberries. And Uncle Al didn't eat smoothies.)

The pasta was one of two meals we had on those days. Later in the day, we'd also have hot dogs, sausages, potato salad, macaroni salad, tossed salad, fresh fruit, chips, and pretzels. In reality, if you said it was really one continuous meal instead of two, you wouldn't be far from the truth. The eating might be broken up by a little nap or a game of softball. But mostly, we ate.

One other noneating diversion was card playing, specifically pinochle, played exclusively by the men. (The women occasionally played gin rummy or canasta.) It was a sign of emerging manhood when you were old enough to play pinochle with the men. But you had to have your wits about you when you played with my father and Uncle Charlie. Dad was a very good pinochle player, who would yell at you for playing the wrong card. Uncle Charlie was an excellent pinochle player, who was always telling you, in unmistakably superior tones, how many points you were going to make and what cards you should and shouldn't have played. I recognized early on that I didn't need that kind of abuse, so I satisfied myself with observing or resting until the next wave of hunger came over me.

I do remember one picnic when we didn't have pasta. On that occasion, the aunts and uncles had decided to have steaks. Unfortunately, they made the mistake of giving the task of bringing the grill to my cheese-phobic Big Uncle Al. Despite his ticks about cheese and strawberries, Uncle Al was a kind and generous man with a quirky (as in "huh?") sense of humor. But he was never the most punctual person in the world.

My father was not amused by Uncle Al's poky style. Though annoying, it was usually harmless. Now, it threatened something near and dear to my father's heart—his dinner. In general, Dad was not a man to be trifled with for any reason. But eating was among his more serious pursuits. Though a quiet man, he would occasionally erupt like a previously dormant volcano. He had such a physical presence that no one dared challenge him (except my mother, who, in her own way, was fearless). And so, when Dad bellowed, "Where the hell is Al!?" we knew he was about to take matters into his own massive hands.

Dad made his own grill out of the tire irons from all the cars of the people who did show up on time. The steaks cooked just fine; they wouldn't have dared otherwise. Uncle Al made it just in time for dessert. My father took this incident as a bad omen. And so he "made the cross" (see below), and we returned to our beloved pasta thereafter. The only exception made to the picnic pasta rule was fried chicken. Really, it was fried and baked ("fraked"?) chicken. Mom would do a whole batch (10 chickens for 22 people) and put them in large roasting pans. Though it wasn't pasta, it was still good. And you didn't have to wait for Uncle Al to bring the frying pans.

A word about "making the cross." When there was something or someone Dad would not put up with anymore, Dad would hold out his left hand with the palm open and slightly facing him. Then he would make a cross in that palm with the fingertips of his right hand. We all knew that was the death sentence—figuratively, of course—for whatever or whoever had gone too far. This ritual was so profound that my wife, who never met my father, now makes the cross the way Dad did. Fortunately, I have never been the object of that hex.

I was often reminded of the old family picnics when I saw people setting up lawn chairs and volleyball nets along Kelly and Martin Luther King Drives in Philadelphia on Sunday mornings when I ran the 8.2-mile loop around those drives as training for my three marathons. Judging from the amount of food and equipment, a lot of people seemed to have had the same philosophy about picnics as my family had. But today, people bring a lot more paraphernalia with them, like wide-screen TVs.

While I enjoyed those picnics as a kid, the idea of schlepping all that food and equipment to the park for a relaxing afternoon outdoors strikes me as a little looney. For me, picnics are an opportunity to commune with nature and friends in a quiet pastoral setting, as far away as possible from the blare of boom boxes and the cloying wafts of cheap barbeque sauces. Anything more complicated than a good loaf of bread, some salami, cheese, olives, and fruit isn't worth taking. And no tubs of ice with cans of beer, soda, and iced tea either. Just a bottle of wine or spring water; that's it. Then a little nap, some softball, maybe a hand or two of pinochle …

Big Aunt Jo and Big Uncle Al

PICNIC CHICKEN

1 tablespoon paprika

1 tablespoon garlic powder

3–4 teaspoons salt, or to taste

1–1 1/2 teaspoons pepper

About 6 pounds frying
  chicken or chicken parts,
  16 serving pieces in all

2 cups flour

1/2 cup olive oil

1/2 cup canola oil

1. Mix the paprika, garlic powder, salt, and pepper together. Use half to rub onto the chicken. Mix the other half with the flour in a sturdy paper bag.

2. Put a large cast-iron or similar skillet over high heat. Add both oils.

3. While the oil gets hot but not smoking, put the chicken, one piece at a time, in the bag with the flour mixture. Shake to make sure the piece is well coated. Remove, shaking off any excess flour, and add to the skillet. Add as many pieces to the frying pan as possible without crowding.

4. Heat the oven to 350 degrees. When each piece is well browned on both sides but not completely cooked, transfer to a roasting pan. Cook, covered, in the oven for one hour. Serve warm or at room temperature. Serves 8-10.

POTATO SALAD

Mom used regular all-purpose potatoes and peeled them after they were cooked. I prefer the rustic look (and added nutritional value) of unpeeled red-skinned potatoes, especially if they are new. Just give them a good scrubbing. Mom usually put a radish rose or two on top of the potato salad in addition to the pepper ring and grated carrots. They're not hard to make, and you can learn quickly from a YouTube video.

3 pounds red-jacketed potatoes, unpeeled and scrubbed

Salt

2 small green bell peppers

4 ribs celery

1 small sweet onion

1 medium-size carrot

1 1/2 cups mayonnaise

1 cup sour cream

4 hard-boiled eggs

White pepper to taste

Paprika

Radish rose (optional)

1. If necessary, cut any potatoes that are too large so all the pieces are relatively even in size. Put the potatoes in a pan large enough to hold all of them and cover with water. Add a tablespoon of salt, stir, and cook at a gentle boil until they can be pierced with a fork, about 15 minutes. (Be careful not to overcook.) Drain, and set aside to cool. When cool enough to handle, cut into 3/8-inch slices or 1/2-inch cubes. (Do not peel.)

2. While the potatoes are cooling, cut the bell peppers into 1/4-inch pieces, except for 3 rings (which will be used for garnish). Put the peppers in a large mixing bowl. Cut the celery into 1/4-inch-wide crescents. Add to the bowl. Finely chop the onion. Add to the bowl. Grate the carrot. Add half to the bowl. Set aside the rest with the pepper rings.

3. Add the potatoes to the mixing bowl. Season with salt and pepper, and mix well. Combine the mayonnaise and sour cream. Add to the bowl, and mix well. Quarter three of the eggs and gently fold them in. Refrigerate at least two hours.

4. Check the potato salad for mayonnaise and seasoning, and adjust to suit your taste. Put the potato salad in a serving bowl. Garnish with remaining grated carrot, green pepper rings, the remaining hard-boiled egg (sliced), and a dusting of paprika. Serves 10–12.

MACARONI SALAD

Use the same ingredients as in the potato salad recipe, with two exceptions: cook 1 pound elbow macaroni instead of the potatoes, and add 2 (6 1/2 ounce) cans of tuna fish in water (drained) when assembling the salad.

ITALIAN SWEET SAUSAGE

This is not the same sausage we used for our picnics. Mom started making it in the early 1970s. She got the recipe from her friend Mrs. Zarcone, whose husband was a butcher. Sausage casings are available at most butcher shops, especially the ones that make their own sausages. The butcher shop should also grind the pork for you. Ask the butcher how much sausage casings you'll need for the amount of pork and cheese in the recipe. He should give you more than what you'll really need in case some of the casings break.

Mom's original recipe said merely "cheese." When I asked her to be more specific, she said, "You pick up a handful." When I pressed further, she said, "Oh, about a half a pound." I use the second-largest holes on a box grater.

5–6 pounds pork butt, ground

2 tablespoons fennel seeds

Salt and pepper to taste

1 cup warm water

1/2 pound Romano cheese, coarsely grated or cut into small cubes

Sausage casings, soaked 4 hours or overnight

1. Mix all ingredients together, except sausage casings. Set aside for 1/2 hour.

2. Gently pat dry the sausage casings, leaving a good bit of moisture. This will help lubricate them as you slide casings over the tube of the sausage attachment of a standing mixer, like a Kitchen Aid. Push as much of the casings over the tube as you can, leaving about 4 inches dangling. (The pork mixture will flow into the casings.)

3. Tie the end of the casings into a knot. Turn the machine on and slowly push the pork mixture through the tube and into the casings, making one long rope.

4. Mark off about five inches along the rope (or however long you want your links to be). Then pinch and twist to tie off a link. Turn a few times in the same direction. Do the same for the next link, except twist and turn in the opposite direction. Continue alternating until the sausage links are completed. Prick both sides of each link a few times with a sterilized pin or a thin needle. (This will help keep the sausage from bursting as it cooks.)

5. You can cook sausages on a grill, but be careful. They are delicate. No more than medium heat. Or cook them in a skillet, with 1/2 inch of cold water. Bring to a boil over medium heat, and simmer until water evaporates, turning the sausages halfway through. Add a little olive oil before the water completely evaporates to help the sausages brown. (You can also brown the sausages on the grill.)

TRADITIONS

"Why do we do it?" says Tevye in *Fiddler on the Roof*. "I'll tell you why. I don't know. But it's a tradition." Just like Tevye, Mom recalled many traditions, rituals, and superstitions, the origins and raisons d'être of which have been lost or obscured over time. Once, Mom told me that she never ate turkey as a child. Her family ate capon instead, even for Thanksgiving. "Why?" I asked. "I don't know," Mom replied, "but it tasted good anyway."

Some of our family traditions go back to "the old country," in this case, Sicily. Grandma looked every bit the quintessential Sicilian widow. She always dressed in black—except when she was peculiarly decked out in a pink dress in her coffin in the funeral parlor. Her gray hair was in a bun, and she spoke virtually no English. Almost everything she did told you that the fact she was in America and not her native Sicily was a mere formality. When we lived upstairs from Grandma, I was able to observe many of her now-extinct rituals and superstitions.

Each spring, Grandma would run through every room of the house, waving a branch from our grape arbor, shouting something in Italian, which, like most things she said, I didn't understand. I assumed it had something to do with the beginning of the growing season for the grapes, a plea to God for a good crop, perhaps.

When I got older, Mom told me it was connected with Easter. In those days, the Resurrection of Jesus, and thus, the end of the Lenten period of fasting, was celebrated at 12:01 p.m. On the day before Easter Sunday (aka Holy Saturday). At the appointed hour, the church bells rang, and Grandma would grab her branch and shout the rough Italian equivalent of "Devil, leave our house. Jesus, come in."

One of the more bizarre superstitions was the *malocchio*—the evil eye. This was the Italian version of the voodoo doll but without the doll or the pins. Someone who was envious of your good fortune could put a curse on you that would make you physically ill. As strange as it sounds, it really did happen. Once, Mom was so afflicted because, she assumed, someone was jealous of her wonderful family. (Well, who wouldn't be?) Aunt Sandy had the antidote. She would say a special set of prayers while holding Mom's hand. There was some anointing with olive oil too—actually blended olive oil; 100% olive oil was too expensive. This isn't as funny as it seems. John Ashcroft, the evangelical attorney general under George W. Bush, anointed himself with Crisco oil when he took office.

The evil eye isn't limited to Sicily or even Italy. In some of Daniel Silva's spy novels, he writes about an old woman in Corsica who sounds a lot like my grandmother. She helps people get rid of the evil eye with prayers and olive oil. And when I was on a press trip to Turkey, I purchased a round silvery plaque with a blue eye on it, which is supposed to ward off the curse. (Turks believe that blue is the color for good luck. Many Turks wear jewelry with blue-eye amulets.)

St. Blaise Day on February 3 was another important ritual in my family and among Catholics in general. St. Blaise lived in the late third and early fourth centuries and was a physician before being made Bishop of Sebaste in Armenia. He was persecuted by the Romans (who had not yet adopted Christianity as their official religion) and fled to a cave in the mountains. One day, a woman brought him a boy who was at the point of death because of a fish bone stuck in his throat. By saving the boy's life, St. Blaise became the patron saint of, among other things, "those who suffer afflictions of the throat." While awaiting his execution (in this case, by beheading), legend tells us a woman brought him two candles to brighten up his dark and dreary dungeon.

Catholics went to church on St. Blaise Day to have their throats blessed. This was done to ward off prospective throat maladies, including but not limited to lodged fish bones. In keeping with the legend, the priest would put two crossed and tied candles against your throat. The priest said a few prayers, and, presto, your throat was blessed until next year, or 5,000 miles, whichever came first.

Apparently, my family did not think that the St. Blaise candelabra was sufficient insurance. Grandma also made St. Blaise cookies, which we were supposed to eat right after we came home from getting our throats blessed at church. These cookies were very bland and unappetizing, but you weren't supposed to enjoy them anyway. I chewed the cookie reverentially and said a few prayers. I still got sore throats, but I never choked on a fish bone, though, as I've noted, we didn't eat a lot of fish.

I think St. Blaise was canonized at the suggestion of someone who was in charge of public relations for the Pope. "Your Holiness, we've got to do something about these complaints of people getting fish bones stuck in their throats. We've got them eating fish on Fridays, but the fishing lobby is getting nervous. If we don't do something about these fish bones, people will start going back to salami. I have an idea."

Many ethnic and religious traditions involve food. The Greeks in New York celebrate January 1, St. Basil's Day, by placing a coin inside a large cake. The person who gets the coin in his or her piece of cake is supposed to have good luck for the year, unless they get the coin stuck in their throat. (Where is St. Blaise when you need him?)

Eating the tail or butt—or *culo*, in Italian—of the turkey on Thanksgiving is certainly not an Italian custom. But it was a Gugino family tradition. When the turkey was done, Mom presented Dad with what we called the "couli." This signaled the beginning of Thanksgiving dinner, much like a celebrity throwing out the first ball on opening day in Major League Baseball.

After Dad died, my brothers and I would vie for the couli, much to the bewilderment of our spouses. You must remember that these are the same guys who fought over the heart, gizzard, and unborn eggs of Mom's soup chicken. The soup chicken also provided us with another ritual, the wishbone. After the chicken was eaten, the wishbone was dried in the oven, and two of us made a wish. I think we wished for chickens with more hearts and gizzards and turkeys with more coulis.

On New Year's Eve, the family had a tradition of watching Guy Lombardo on television while the adults drank highballs and played cards. The kids played a card game called seven and a half, a variation of blackjack. We played for pennies and loved it. After the stroke of twelve, Mom served pizza, sausage, olive salad, and holiday cookies. Though the foods remain, the rest of that New Year's Eve ritual has gone the way of Ben Grauer (who narrated the New Year's ball coming down in Times Square).

Mom made thick-dough pizza before anyone ever heard the term "Sicilian-style" pizza. We never had any other kind, except on those rare occasions when one of my brothers and I would buy a pizza with friends after a ball game. I used to think, *Why does everyone else make this weird thin pizza?*

Mom made her pizza in rectangular black tins, never fewer than two at a time. The sauce was homemade from the tomatoes she canned in late summer. What could be better? I'm happy to say that I have had these very same black tins since Mom stopped making pizza in her late 80s.

You'll notice in her pizza recipe that Mom automatically put bits of anchovies on the dough before adding the sauce. This way, the anchovies have a subtler flavor that even anchovy haters, like my wife, Mary, can tolerate. If, however, the mere idea of anchovies is abhorrent to you, please feel free to omit them, or put them in the sauce, where their flavor will barely be noticed.

When Mom made pizza, she always seemed to have some dough left over. (I think she planned it that way.) The plain dough was fried in oil and sprinkled with sugar while still hot. We called it *pizza fritte* ("freet," which means fried and should, grammatically, be "fritta"). It's hard to imagine that something so simple could taste so good.

It may seem ironic that I, the only childless sibling, want to maintain traditions probably more than anyone else in the family. (I'm sure Mom would have put out a St. Joseph's table spread the size of Yankee Stadium if Mary and I ever had decided to have kids.) But life doesn't always get tied up into nice, neat little packages. For example, Jill, Russell's wife, and the most fecund of my sisters-in-law, is a person who thinks pizza is the kind of food that should be microwaved directly from the freezer—the supermarket freezer. I had three sisters-in-law courtesy of my older brother, Frank. To my knowledge, none of them, including Patti, his current wife, has ever made Mom's pizza.

Sam cutting Mom's pizza in her kitchen

MOM'S SICILIAN-STYLE PIZZA

Dough

3 3/4 cups flour

1 package dry yeast

1/2 teaspoon sugar

2 teaspoons salt

3 tablespoons olive oil

Warm water (about 100 degrees), about 1 1/2 cups

Sauce

2 tablespoons olive oil

1 small onion (about 6 ounces), sliced thinly

1 (28-ounce) can plum tomatoes, chopped*

1 teaspoon dried oregano

2 tablespoons chopped fresh basil (or Italian parsley)

1 bay leaf

Salt and pepper to taste

Assembly and Toppings

2 anchovy fillets

1/2 cup grated cheese, equal parts Parmigiano and Romano

6–8 ounces shredded mozzarella cheese**

25–30 thin slices of pepperoni (optional)

1. If you are using a standing mixer with a dough hook, combine the flour, yeast, sugar, and salt in the bowl of the mixer. Whisk in 2 tablespoons of the olive oil. (If mixing by hand, combine in a bowl large enough to incorporate all the dough ingredients.)

2. With the mixer running at slow speed (or by hand, if not using a mixer), gradually add 1 cup of the warm water. Stop two or three times to scrape any dough from the sides of the bowl. Continue to add the warm water, a tablespoon at a time, until you have a somewhat sticky dough. Add 1–2 tablespoons of flour if the dough is too sticky.

3. Let the dough hook knead the dough at medium speed for 1–2 minutes, or knead by hand for about 5 minutes. Let the dough rest for 10 minutes.

4. Knead the dough again with the dough hook for a few minutes or until a smooth mass is achieved. (Or by hand, which will take about 5 minutes.) Put the remaining tablespoon of olive oil in a clean mixing bowl large enough to accommodate risen dough. Coat the dough with the olive oil inside the bowl, and turn the dough upside down so that the smoothest part is on top. Cover with a cloth, and let rise 90 minutes in a warm, draft-free area.

5. Meanwhile, prepare the sauce. Put a large, heavy-bottom saucepan over medium heat. Add the oil. Add the onion, and sauté until the onion is very soft but not browned. Add the remaining ingredients. Simmer for about 30 minutes or until the sauce is quite thick. Let cool to room temperature.

6. Punch the dough down to deflate. Form into a ball, and let rise again, covered, for 90 minutes in a warm, draft-free area.

7. Punch the dough down again. Then roll it out evenly to approximately the size of an 11x17-inch pan. By hand, stretch and press the dough to exactly fit the pan. Cover

and let rest for 10 minutes.

8. Meanwhile, heat the oven to 400 degrees.

9. Break the anchovies into small pieces, and dot the dough evenly with them. Add the sauce, and spread evenly. Sprinkle with the grated cheese, then top with the mozzarella.

10. Bake in the oven for 20–25 minutes, until the bottom is light brown. Add on the pepperoni (if using) during the last 5 minutes. Serves 3–4.

*You can also pulse the tomatoes in a food processor, or crush them in the pot with a potato masher.

**Putting the mozzarella in the freezer for a half hour or so makes shredding easier. If you don't have a shredding attachment to your food processor, I recommend buying mozzarella already shredded. It covers the top of the pizza more evenly.

PIZZA FRITTE

Leftover dough from pizza or from billulata (See Without Bread chapter on page 75.)

Vegetable oil (not olive)

Granulated sugar (not powdered)

1. Roll out dough, or stretch it out with your fingers to make pieces anywhere from 1 1/2 inches square to 3 inches square. (The shape need not be uniform. You could make rounds with the mouth of a jar. Or let kids make their own.) It should be about 1/4 inch thick or less.

2. Put a cast-iron or other heavy-bottom skillet over medium-high heat. Add vegetable oil to a depth of 1/4 inch.

3. Meanwhile, put the sugar in a bowl large enough to hold the fried pieces of dough.

4. When the oil in the skillet is hot but not smoking, add the dough. Cook until golden brown on both sides, in batches, if necessary. Put the browned pieces into the bowl of sugar as they finish cooking. (Do not drain on paper towels.) Coat them with the sugar, put them on a warm platter, and eat at once.

CASSATA

Cassata is a traditional Sicilian cake made on special occasions. Mom made it infrequently because she said it was "so expensive." It's not really that expensive, even when you use liqueur to soak the cake.

When I made cassata at Vincenzo's, my first restaurant, it was with pound cake in a loaf shape. I frosted the cake with chocolate instead of whipped cream.

Sponge Cake

A few tablespoons of softened butter or butter-flavored spray

A few tablespoons of flour

6 eggs, separated

2 tablespoons cold water

1 cup sugar

2 teaspoons lemon rind

1 tablespoon fresh lemon juice

1 cup sifted cake flour

1/4 teaspoon salt

1. Heat the oven to 325 degrees. Grease a tube pan with butter or spray; dust with flour, shaking out any excess.
2. Beat the egg yolks, water, and sugar until they become thick and custard-colored.
3. Stir in the lemon rind and lemon juice.
4. Gradually mix in the flour.
5. In a separate bowl, beat the egg whites with salt until stiff peaks form. Gently fold the egg whites into the flour mixture in stages. Don't overmix.
6. Pour the batter into the tube pan. Bake for 45 minutes or until a tester comes out clean and the cake pulls away from the sides of the pan. (You can make the filling while the cake bakes.)
7. Invert the tube pan onto a plate, and let cool. Remove the cake from the pan. Put the cake into the freezer to firm up before cutting.

Filling and Frosting

1 pound whole-milk ricotta

3/4 cup plus 2 tablespoons powdered sugar, divided

1/4 teaspoon cinnamon

1/2 teaspoon vanilla

1/2 teaspoon almond extract

1/4 cup chopped walnuts or pecans

1/4 cup chopped candied fruit

2 tablespoons chopped semisweet chocolate*

1 pint heavy cream

1. To make the ricotta smoother, put it through a fine sieve using the back of a large spoon or crank it through a food mill into a mixing bowl.

2. Add the 3/4 cup of powdered sugar and mix well. Mix in all the other ingredients, except the remaining powdered sugar and heavy cream.

3. Whip the cream with the remaining powdered sugar until stiff peaks form.

4. Fold 3/4 cup of the whipped cream into the ricotta mixture. Refrigerate the ricotta mixture and the remaining whipped cream.

To Assemble

Sponge cake

1/4–1/2 cup orange-flavored liqueur, like triple sec or Cointreau**

Ricotta filling

Reserved whipped cream

Whole candied fruit and pieces of chocolate for decoration

1. Slice sponge cake across with a serrated knife to form 3 rings of roughly equal thickness.

2. With 4 (2-inch-wide) strips of waxed paper, form an overlapping square covering the edges of a serving plate. Put bottom ring of the sponge cake on the plate so that the waxed paper covers the area from just underneath the cake to the edge of the plate so that no bare plate shows. Sprinkle the cake with one-third of the orange liqueur.

3. Spread half of the filling on the bottom layer of the cake. Place the second layer on top, and repeat the process.

4. Put the top layer on, and sprinkle with the remaining liqueur. Frost the entire cake with the whipped cream. Decorate with whole candied fruit and chocolate. Slide the waxed paper strips off the plate. Refrigerate for several hours or overnight in the coldest part of the refrigerator. Serves 8–10.

* You can buy a hunk of chocolate and chop it for the filling and decoration or use chocolate morsels.

** Mom didn't use liqueur, but I think it makes a better cake. You may also want to try another kind, like maraschino or amaretto.

CANNOLI

Cannoli was one of Mom's three favorite desserts, the others being maple walnut ice cream and watermelon. Every so often, Dad would bring home a box of cannoli from Muscarella's Bakery to surprise Mom. Though they were good, the Muscarella cannoli had the same problem most store-bought cannoli have. The cannoli shells are almost always filled when you buy them, which means the shells are probably soggy from the moisture of the filling by the time you eat them. Whether you are making them at home or buying them at a bakery, fill the shells (or have them filled) as close to eating them as possible.

The metal tubes for making the cannoli shells, about 5 inches long, can be purchased at most cookware shops or online. The cannoli in the following recipe are smaller than commercial cannoli. You may, therefore, want to allow two per person.

Filling

1 pound ricotta
1 cup heavy cream
1 cup powdered sugar
1/4 teaspoon cinnamon
1/2 teaspoon vanilla

1/2 teaspoon almond extract
2–4 tablespoons rum, orange
  liqueur, or brandy
1/4 cup chopped walnuts or
  pecans

1/4 cup chopped candied
  fruit
2 tablespoons chopped
  semisweet chocolate

1. Wrap the ricotta in cheesecloth, and put it on a strainer over a bowl to allow excess moisture to drain, refrigerated, for 2 hours. (While you wait for the ricotta to strain, you can make the cannoli shells. See below.)

2. Put the strained ricotta in a mixing bowl. Beat with an electric mixer, gradually adding the heavy cream. Then add 3/4 cup of the powdered sugar until you have a thick, smooth mixture. Then add the cinnamon, vanilla extract, almond extract, and rum (or other liquor), and mix thoroughly. Fold in the nuts, fruit, and chocolate. Refrigerate until you are ready to fill the cannoli shells.

Shells

1 tablespoon high-quality
  shortening
1 1/2 tablespoons sugar
1 egg, separated

1/2 teaspoon vanilla
1/4 cup warm water
1 "shot" (1 1/2 ounces) of
  whiskey or brandy

2 cups flour
Canola or vegetable oil for
  deep frying

1. Cream the shortening. Then add the sugar and mix well. Add the egg yolk and vanilla and continue mixing. Add the water and whiskey and mix thoroughly.

2. Gradually add 1 3/4 cups of the flour until it is fully incorporated. Add some or all of the remaining flour, as needed. Form the dough into a ball and roll out very thin (1/8 inch or less). With the mouth of a jar or a cookie cutter, 3 to 3 1/2 inches in diameter, cut out rounds from the dough. Gather the leftover scraps of dough, and form them into a ball. Roll out the dough and cut into as many circles as you can. You should have about 20 dough circles.

3. Whisk the egg white briefly in a small bowl. Gently stretch or roll each dough round into an oblong shape. Before you wrap the dough around the metal cannoli tubes, brush or use your finger to dab a little of the egg white on the part of the dough that will be overlapped. Wrap the dough, lengthwise, around one of the cannoli tubes. Press just firmly enough to form a good seal. (If you press too firmly, it may be difficult to slide the cooked shell off the tube. If you press too gently, the seal may break.)

4. Pour the oil into a frying pan to a depth of 1/2 inch. Heat over moderately high flame until hot but not smoking, about 350 degrees.

5. Add the shells without crowding the pan. Fry until golden brown on all sides. Turn periodically with tongs to brown evenly. They should be an even deep-golden color.

6. Put the shells on paper towels to absorb any grease. When cool enough to handle, gently remove the shell from the tube. (If the shells don't come off easily, give the ends of the tubes a few gentle but firm taps on the counter.) Once cooled, shells can be kept in a covered tin or plastic container for a few days at room temperature. Makes about 20 cannoli shells.

Assembly

1. Put the filling in a pastry bag with an opening large enough to fill the cannoli. (You can also put the filling in a zipper freezer bag and snip off one corner with scissors.)

2. Pipe the filling into the cannoli. Dust with remaining powdered sugar, and serve. About 20 cannoli or 10 servings.

HOW ABOUT A CUP OF COFFEE?

"How about a cup of coffee?" Mom would say to anyone who came into our house. Attila the Hun could come to the door, and Mom would say, "How about a cup of coffee before you go out pillaging in the neighborhood?"

During holidays, she might say, "How about a highball?" or "How about some schnapps?" People might decline both, but then Mom would say, "At least have a cup of coffee," as if to imply that to leave our house without ingesting something would be an insult.

We drank coffee with or after breakfast, lunch, and dinner. "It just rounds out a meal," Mom often said. After dinner, especially in the summer or on a Friday night, we'd have coffee with some dessert Mom made or with some of Aunt Sandy's cookies.

Mom had a perpetual pot of coffee on the stove, either brewing, warming, or cold and ready to be heated up. It was a comforting symbol, like votive candles always lit in the church. We would sit around the kitchen table for hours, drinking coffee and talking about everything from school to sports, politics, or the occasional family scandal.

No one drank hot tea, incidentally. That you drank with honey and lemon when you had a cold, unless it was summer. Then Mom had a perpetual pitcher of iced tea in the refrigerator (or, as my uncle Ben used to call it, "the Frigidaire").

Decaffeinated coffee was out of the question. Oh, we heard rumors of some strange beverage called Sanka, but they were as remote as the latest diet craze. I guess it wasn't until Robert Young annoyed the nation by asking in a television commercial, "Hey, why so tense?" that the issue of caffeine became something of which we took notice.

When I was growing up, the only health concern connected with coffee was uttered by Aunt Sandy, who would routinely admonish us about drinking any coffee at all. In her all-too-familiar raspy whine, she'd say, "You can't drink coffee; you're too young. It'll stunt your growth." We drank it anyway, as early in my youth as I can remember, without any ill effects. Russ and I both reached close to 6 feet 4 inches. Frank was 6 feet 1, and Maria is 5 feet 9. So much for warning labels.

As a concession to our age and an appeasement to Aunt Sandy, we put lots of milk in our coffee. I can remember going downstairs on Fargo Avenue to Grandma's after dinner and having coffee and milk heated in a saucepan with lots of sugar. I often thought that was a little weird, like so many other things we did, until I drank the same concoction all over Italy, where the Italians called it caffe latte. The French even made it chic by calling it café au lait.

I would drink caffe latte while I attempted to teach Grandma English, and she did the same to me with Italian. Grandma knew about ten words of English then. And when she died, she knew just about the same number. She was equally unsuccessful in teaching me Italian, or at least the Sicilian dialect, which isn't necessarily the same thing.

Since my caffe latte days, the concern over caffeine has increased so that it's now up there right behind salt, sugar, saturated fat, and, for some people, carbs. But why should I listen to these health concerns any more than I listened to Aunt Sandy? My paternal grandfather used to put coffee over his corn flakes. He lived to be 94. Maybe that's a coincidence. And maybe the corn flakes somehow neutralized the caffeine. But you've got to wonder.

These days, my morning coffee is a double cappuccino, which I make for my wife and me. I've used several different espresso machines over the years like Gaggia and Saeco. The current one is a Breville. I also make drip coffee during the day from beans freshly roasted by a local outfit. (I also roasted my own beans at one time for a *Wine Spectator* column, though I can't say they were any better than professionally roasted beans.)

Though I do remember the occasional percolated coffee, Mom's go-to coffee maker was this very '50s-looking coffeepot divided into two sections. The top section had a compartment for the grounds. There were tiny holes for the hot water to pass through. She had this pot for 38 years. After about 20 of those years, the handle on the bottom section broke. The company replaced it, free of charge. Sometime later, Mom told me she didn't know what she would do if it happened again because the company went out of business, probably from replacing parts for free for two decades. (Mom had a whole cupboard full of pots from that company that also lasted seemingly forever. Now I have one of them. It's the pot in which she used to make lamb stew.)

Here are some tips for making better, if not great, coffee. And don't worry about stunting your growth.

SIX STEPS TO GREAT COFFEE

1. Buy coffee beans from a roaster, either local or one who sells by mail, who tells you on the package when the beans were roasted, how they were roasted (light, medium, dark), and where the beans came from.

2. Store the beans, well-sealed, in a dark, cool, and dry place, and grind only what you need.

3. Grind the beans in a burr grinder that, unlike a chopper, creates even grounds.

4. Use only cold, filtered tap water or spring water to brew coffee.

5. If using an electric drip coffeemaker, it should be one that produces enough power to sufficiently heat the water, at least 1250 watts. The water should be around 200 degrees, but no hotter than 205 and no lower than 195. (Most coffee makers don't have that power, so the water never gets hot enough.) The simplest (and cheapest) way to make drip coffee is to boil water in a kettle and manually pour the water over the ground coffee, in a cone lined with filter paper that sits securely on a container, preferably an insulated one.

6. Keep the brewed coffee in an insulated container. Never heat already-brewed coffee. It breaks down the flavor. Just keep it as hot as you can once it's made. Consume it within 30 to 60 minutes.

EPILOGUE

From the time I became the restaurant critic for the *Philadelphia Daily News* in 1986 until I retired in 2016, the third most frequently asked question of me —after "Have you been to any good restaurants lately?" and "How come you're so thin?"—was "How did you get so involved with food?" I usually responded by saying I had a long and dedicated history of eating.

That early oral conditioning had more of an effect on me than I realized. But rather than channel it into mere eating, I parlayed it into an occupation that was the envy of many, including some who had pretty good jobs themselves. Once, while joining me in "research" at a restaurant, *Philadelphia Daily News* film critic Ben Yagoda turned to me with a satisfied mouthful of food and a green-eyed look and said, "Boy, do you have a great job."

I responded with surprise and thinly veiled self-approbation. "Gee, Ben, I thought *you* had the great job."

The irony is that, despite the common assumption, being a restaurant critic was hard work. There were more than a few times that I dreaded going out to eat. This applied to other critics as well. And not just restaurant critics. When I was living in Manhattan, I was at a dinner at the James Beard House, seated next to a *New York Times* theater critic, who moaned about how much bad theater he had to sit through before he got to see just one good play.

Those few instances of dread aside, I've always loved eating and the camaraderie and conversation that go with it. And since my first published article in the early 1980s, I've loved writing. But the one thing that makes me most like my mother, without whom this book would not have been written, is my love of cooking. Cooking for friends. Cooking for family. And, most of all, cooking for my wife, Mary.

I have mentioned elsewhere in this book that my wife's exposure to food and cooking was very limited when she was growing up. She was convinced that her mother didn't like to cook and did it only out of her obligation as a wife and mother. This clearly rubbed off on Mary, who would settle for a dinner of microwaved frozen brussels sprouts when I met her.

Mary saw no need to cook after we began seeing each other. And since we moved in together in 1975—we got married on our tenth anniversary of not being married—she has never cooked a full meal, for me or for herself. A sandwich here and a bowl of popcorn there. But never a meal. And why should she? She's got me. And, with some exceptions, I've been happy to oblige. (I like to tell people that I'd trust Mary with my life, but I wouldn't trust her to cook dinner for me.)

Occasionally, though, when dinner is ready, Mary may revert to her old self and say, "I'm just not hungry." That's when one of Mom's old adages comes in handy, and I say, "Eat! You'll get hungry."

PANTRY

There are a lot of ingredients Mom used for various reasons but mostly because she was always conscious of cost, or in some cases, taste. Olive oil is a case in point. Mom never used 100 percent olive oil because it was too expensive. It was always a blend of olive oil and vegetable oil. Don't even think about extra-virgin olive oil (or cold-pressed or organic). Not only did few people, including Italian Americans, know about extra-virgin olive oil back then, but the taste would have been too strong. Here are pantry items not just for the recipes in this book but many other recipes as well:

Beans

I use canned beans almost exclusively because the quality is generally good, and I don't have the patience to cook dried beans from scratch. I usually keep five or six varieties, but I mainly use chickpeas and cannellini beans.

Bread crumbs

I use panko, the Japanese-style bread crumbs (whole wheat, if I can find it), which have a drier and flakier consistency than regular bread crumbs. They absorb less oil and make for lighter and crunchier fried food. I also keep flavored panko bread crumbs, in case I'm too lazy to add the seasonings myself.

Butter

I use Land O'Lakes brand, unsalted, so I can add the salt to a dish myself. (Buy it on sale, and freeze it.)

Cheese

There are two grating cheeses I always keep in my refrigerator. I buy them by the piece and grate them as needed.

- **Parmigiano-Reggiano**. The real deal cow's-milk cheese from Italy, not the ersatz grating cheeses labeled "Parmesan." Though there are quite a few brands or producers of Parmigiano-Reggiano (which I refer to as just Parmigiano in this book), all must have the name stamped on the rind. Grana Padano is a Parmigiano-style cheese that comes from the same region in Italy (Emilia-Romagna) and can be as good as Parmigiano-Reggiano. (Or at least most folks can't tell the difference.) It's usually cheaper, too.

- **Pecorino-Romano**. Sometimes just called Romano, which is how I refer to it in this book, this sheep's-milk cheese has a higher butterfat content than Parmigiano. (*Pecorino* means "sheep," and there are other types of pecorino cheeses, such as pecorino Toscano.) But this is offset by its sharper, earthier taste. Thus, it is typically used in more rustic dishes from southern Italy. The ubiquitous Locatelli brand is too salty for my taste. I prefer Fulvi. This is the cheese we used on pasta dishes.

Flour

Unless otherwise specified, use all-purpose flour.

Olive oil

I use two kinds of olive oil, both extra-virgin. One (usually Pompeian, Bertolli, or Filippo Berio brands) is less intense and cheaper. I use it for cooking and marinades. More expensive oils—often from Italy, Greece, and Spain—have deeper, more concentrated flavors and are used in smaller amounts to finish dishes like salads and pastas. The brands I buy vary, depending on availability and price. Most of the recipes in this book use the former. When the latter is called for, I'll indicate "high quality."

Other oils

When a neutral oil is called for, I use canola or grapeseed oil. Grapeseed oil has a higher smoke point, which means it is better at higher temperatures. Keep all oils in a cool, dark place. Never refrigerate.

Olives

For dishes like Mom's olive salad, I use Cerignola and Castelvetrano Italian green olives, which are sweeter than the Greek varieties Mom used. I keep two kinds of black olives on hand: one oil-cured—that is, not in brine—like those from Morocco or Sicily, and one packed in brine, such as a meaty Greek kalamata.

Seasonings

Fresh herbs

- **Parsley.** I use flat parsley, often referred to as Italian parsley, because it has a more robust flavor.
- **Basil.** As with tomatoes, I buy only locally grown basil in season. Or try to. Sometimes, you have no choice. That's when I'll buy either the hydroponic basil or the basil hermetically sealed in small plastic boxes, where other fresh herbs are sold. Dried basil is not a substitute for fresh, however. You can now buy basil frozen in cubes.
- **Mint.** Mom always grew mint (and basil) in the backyard in two squat tubs made from cut wine barrels. Fresh mint is now widely available in most markets year-round.
- **Sage.** Mom used dried sage because fresh wasn't as available, as it is today. I only use fresh.
- **Thyme and rosemary.** Not used much in Mom's cooking but good to have around and not hard to find.

Dried herbs. Some dried herbs work quite well. Others, like basil and parsley, are a waste of money. Dried herbs in leaf form are always preferable to ground herbs. They last longer and have more punch. But that doesn't mean they last forever. Buy dried herbs in small quantities and date the containers. Keep them no more than one year.

- **Oregano.** I prefer good-quality Mediterranean dried oregano to fresh oregano. It's also more fragrant and less biting than dried Mexican oregano. I buy it in dried bunches, usually from Greece or Sicily. Then I crush some of the dried leaves as needed, removing any bits of stems.
- **Thyme.** Dried is a decent substitute for fresh.
- **Bay leaves.** Essential in many long-cooked dishes. No need to buy fresh, which are hard to get anyway.

Spices. As with dried herbs, buy them in smaller quantities, and date them. Whole spices last longer than ground. (In general, spices last longer than dried herbs.) If possible, grate or grind them as needed.

- **Nutmeg.** I buy whole nutmeg and grate it, as needed, with a rasp grater.

- **Salt**. I use two kinds of salt—coarse kosher salt for dishes that are cooked more than a few minutes, and fine sea salt for finishing cooked dishes or in salads.
- **Pepper**. When "pepper" is listed as an ingredient, it is always freshly ground black pepper.
- **Red pepper flakes**. Made from a variety of dried chiles. Not as hot as some individual ground peppers like cayenne.
- **Garlic**. Buy heads that are tight and firm. Remove any greenish sprouts in the center before chopping. The more garlic is processed, such as finely chopping, grating, or being put through a garlic press, the more garlic flavor is released.

Pasta

I use dried pasta almost exclusively because, in addition to being incredibly convenient, it is consistently good. I prefer pasta imported from Italy, usually Barilla, occasionally the more expensive DeCecco. Mom often used Gioia pasta, which was locally made.

Tomatoes

I'm not too picky about the puree and paste I use in Mom's pasta sauce. Usually, I stick with name brands like Hunts, Contadina, Del Monte, and Cento. For whole tomatoes, I buy the plum-shaped variety from those brands. When I want the taste of the tomatoes to stand out more, I use imported San Marzano tomatoes from the Campania region in Italy. There are also "San Marzano-style" tomatoes, which are usually cheaper but not from the region where real San Marzanos are produced.

Seafood, canned

- **Anchovies**. Buy fillets packed flat in 2-ounce tins, not wrapped around capers.

Vegetables, frozen

- **Frozen peas** are almost universally good quality and what I use in Mom's chicken soup (and many other dishes).

Vinegar

I use apple cider vinegar (usually Bragg's) when a mild vinegar is called for and good-quality white and red wine vinegars for salads and marinades. I also keep two kinds of balsamic vinegars on hand, very much like I do with olive oils. One is a balsamic-style vinegar that is mass produced in several countries and used for marinades and salad dressings. The other is more intense and more expensive from the Emilia-Romagna region in Italy. It is used sparingly, like high-quality olive oil. Once the vinegars are open, I keep them on the shelves of the refrigerator door.

THANK YOU!

Thank you for reading my book. I hope you got as much enjoyment out of these stories and recipes as I did in putting them together for you. Check out my website, samcooks.com, for more information about food and wine.

And don't forget to Eat! You'll Get Hungry.

Sam

ABOUT THE AUTHOR

Sam Gugino was born in Buffalo, NY, and moved to Philadelphia to attend the University of Pennsylvania. An avid amateur cook, he pursued his passion by enrolling at The Restaurant School in Philadelphia, with the goal of opening his own restaurant. After graduation, he became the chef at two critically acclaimed establishments, Vincenzo's and Avanti, with *The Philadelphia Inquirer* praising Vincenzo's as "Where they serve the best Italian food."

Sam combined his culinary expertise with his growing writing career, eventually becoming the restaurant critic for the *Philadelphia Daily News*. He later served as food editor for the *San Jose Mercury News*, where his columns earned national recognition. His work garnered a James Beard Award nomination for a story in *The New York Times* and led to the publication of *Cooking to Beat the Clock*, which was named one of the year's top 10 cookbooks by Amazon. His other notable titles include *Low-Fat Cooking to Beat the Clock*, which was nominated for Cookbook of the Year by the International Association of Culinary Professionals, and *Eat Fresh, Stay Healthy*. He also co-authored Matthew Kenney's *Mediterranean Cooking*.

For two decades, Sam contributed as a columnist and editor for *Wine Spectator* magazine before retiring from his role as a full-time food and wine writer.

At samcooks.com you can read more about Sam's culinary journey and find a wealth of information, such as how to cook delicious meals in fifteen minutes (including Bouillabaisse!), how to pick, store, and prepare fruits and vegetables, and all about wine, including food and wine pairings.

INDEX

The Gugino family before church on Easter Sunday

www.ingramcontent.com/pod-product-compliance
Lightning Source LLC
LaVergne TN
LVHW081327060426
835513LV00012B/1218